# Not On My Watch:

## My Personal Story of Opposing Communism in America

# David Risselada

Cover Design and Interior Layout:  Fred DeRuvo

Cover Image: USA flag and sky © Les Cunliffe

Edited by:  Hannah Brady

**Library of Congress Cataloging-in-Publication Data**

Risselada, David, 1973 –

ISBN 1512182826
EAN-13 978-1512182828

# CONTENTS

## ACKNOWLEDGEMENTS

I would like to thank the following people:

My wife Deborah, for tolerating my constant obsession with politics

David Goestch, of Patriot Update, Fred Brownbill, of the Save America Foundation, and Tim Brown of Freedom Outpost for publishing my rants and making me believe I had something worth saying.

Fred DeRuvo, for encouraging me to write this book, and helping me through the process.

*David Risselada, May 2015*

*I, David Risselada, do solemnly swear that I will support and defend the constitution of The United States against all enemies foreign and domestic, and that I will bear true faith and allegiance to the same...*

## The Constitution of the United States of America

**We the People** of the United States, in Order to form a more perfect Union, establish Justice, insure domestic Tranquility, provide for the common defense, promote the general Welfare, and secure the Blessings of Liberty to ourselves and our Posterity, do ordain and establish this Constitution for the United States of America.

### Article I (Article 1 - Legislative)

#### Section 1

All legislative Powers herein granted shall be vested in a Congress of the United States, which shall consist of a Senate and House of Representatives.

#### Section 2

1: The House of Representatives shall be composed of Members chosen every second Year by the People of the several States, and the Electors in each State shall have the Qualifications requisite for Electors of the most numerous Branch of the State Legislature.

2: No Person shall be a Representative who shall not have attained to the Age of twenty five Years, and been seven Years a Citizen of the United States, and who shall not, when elected, be an Inhabitant of that State in which he shall be chosen.

3: Representatives and direct Taxes shall be apportioned among the several States which may be included within this Union, according to their respective Numbers, which shall be determined by adding to the whole Number of free Persons, including those bound to Service for a Term of Years, and excluding Indians not taxed, three fifths of all other Persons.*2* The actual Enumeration shall be made within three Years after the first Meeting of the Congress of the United States, and within every subsequent Term of ten Years, in such Manner as they shall by Law direct. The Number of Representatives shall not exceed one for every thirty Thousand, but each State shall have at Least one Representative; and until such enumeration shall be made, the State of New Hampshire shall be entitled to choose three, Massachusetts eight, Rhode-Island and Providence Plantations one, Connecticut five, New-York six, New Jersey four, Pennsylvania eight, Delaware one, Maryland six, Virginia ten, North Carolina five, South Carolina five, and Georgia three.

4: When vacancies happen in the Representation from any State, the Executive Authority thereof shall issue Writs of Election to fill such Vacancies.

5: The House of Representatives shall chose their Speaker and other Officers; and shall have the sole Power of Impeachment.

### Section 3

1: The Senate of the United States shall be composed of two Senators from each State, chosen by the Legislature thereof, for six Years; and each Senator shall have one Vote.

2: Immediately after they shall be assembled in Consequence of the first Election, they shall be divided as equally as may be into three Classes. The Seats of the Senators of the first Class shall be vacated at the Expiration of the second Year, of the second Class at the Expiration of the fourth Year, and of the third Class at the Expiration of the sixth Year, so that one third may be chosen every second Year; and if Vacancies happen by Resignation, or otherwise, during the Recess of the Legislature of any State, the Executive thereof may make temporary Appointments until the next Meeting of the Legislature, which shall then fill such Vacancies.

3: No Person shall be a Senator who shall not have attained to the Age of thirty Years, and been nine Years a Citizen of the United States, and who shall not, when elected, be an Inhabitant of that State for which he shall be chosen.

4: The Vice President of the United States shall be President of the Senate, but shall have no Vote, unless they be equally divided.

5: The Senate shall chose their other Officers, and also a President pro tempore, in the Absence of the Vice President, or when he shall exercise the Office of President of the United States.

6: The Senate shall have the sole Power to try all Impeachments. When sitting for that Purpose, they shall be on Oath or Affirmation. When the President of the United States is tried, the Chief Justice shall preside: And no Person shall be convicted without the Concurrence of two thirds of the Members present.

7: Judgment in Cases of impeachment shall not extend further than to removal from Office, and disqualification to hold and enjoy any Office of honor, Trust or Profit under the United States: but the Party convicted shall nevertheless be liable and subject to Indictment, Trial, Judgment and Punishment, according to Law.

### Section 4

1: The Times, Places and Manner of holding Elections for Senators and Representatives, shall be prescribed in each State by the Legislature thereof; but the Congress may at any time by Law make or alter such Regulations, except as to the Places of choosing Senators.

2: The Congress shall assemble at least once in every Year, and such Meeting shall be on the first Monday in December,[5] unless they shall by Law appoint a different Day.

### Section 5

1: Each House shall be the Judge of the Elections, Returns and Qualifications of its own Members, and a Majority of each shall constitute a Quorum to do Business; but a smaller Number may adjourn from day to day, and may be authorized to compel the Attendance of absent Members, in such Manner, and under such Penalties as each House may provide.

2: Each House may determine the Rules of its Proceedings, punish its Members for disorderly Behavior, and, with the Concurrence of two thirds, expel a Member.

3: Each House shall keep a Journal of its Proceedings, and from time to time publish the same, excepting such Parts as may in their Judgment require Secrecy; and the Yeas and Nays of the Members of either House on any question shall, at the Desire of one fifth of those Present, be entered on the Journal.

4: Neither House, during the Session of Congress, shall, without the Consent of the other, adjourn for more than three days, nor to any other Place than that in which the two Houses shall be sitting.

### Section 6

1: The Senators and Representatives shall receive a Compensation for their Services, to be ascertained by Law, and paid out of the Treasury of the United States.[6] They shall in all Cases, except Treason, Felony and Breach of the Peace, be privileged from Arrest during their Attendance at the Session of their respective Houses, and in going to and returning from the same; and for any Speech or Debate in either House, they shall not be questioned in any other Place.

2: No Senator or Representative shall, during the Time for which he was elected, be appointed to any civil Office under the Authority of the United States, which shall have been created, or the Emoluments whereof shall have been increased during such time; and no Person holding any Office under the United States, shall be a Member of either House during his Continuance in Office.

### Section 7

1: All Bills for raising Revenue shall originate in the House of Representatives; but the Senate may propose or concur with Amendments as on other Bills.

2: Every Bill which shall have passed the House of Representatives and the Senate, shall, before it become a Law, be presented to the President of the United States; If he approve he shall sign it, but if not he shall return it, with his Objections to that House in which it shall have originated, who shall enter the Objections at large on their Journal, and proceed to reconsider it. If after such Reconsideration two thirds of that House shall agree to pass the Bill, it shall be sent, together with the Objections, to the other House, by which it shall likewise be reconsidered, and if approved by two thirds of that House, it shall become a Law. But in all such Cases the Votes of both Houses shall be determined by yeas and Nays, and the Names of the Persons voting for and against the Bill shall be entered on the Journal of each House respectively. If any Bill shall not be returned by the President within ten Days (Sundays excepted) after it shall have been presented to him, the same shall be a Law, in like Manner as if he had signed it, unless the Congress by their Adjournment prevent its Return, in which Case it shall not be a Law.

3: Every Order, Resolution, or Vote to which the Concurrence of the Senate and House of Representatives may be necessary (except on a question of Adjournment) shall be presented to the President of the United States; and before the Same shall take Effect, shall be approved by him, or being disapproved by him, shall be repassed by two thirds of the Senate and House of Representatives, according to the Rules and Limitations prescribed in the Case of a Bill.

#### Section 8

1: The Congress shall have Power To lay and collect Taxes, Duties, Imposts and Excises, to pay the Debts and provide for the common Defence and general Welfare of the United States; but all Duties, Imposts and Excises shall be uniform throughout the United States;

2: To borrow Money on the credit of the United States;

3: To regulate Commerce with foreign Nations, and among the several States, and with the Indian Tribes;

4: To establish an uniform Rule of Naturalization, and uniform Laws on the subject of Bankruptcies throughout the United States;

5: To coin Money, regulate the Value thereof, and of foreign Coin, and fix the Standard of Weights and Measures;

6: To provide for the Punishment of counterfeiting the Securities and current Coin of the United States;

7: To establish Post Offices and post Roads;

8: To promote the Progress of Science and useful Arts, by securing for limited Times to Authors and Inventors the exclusive Right to their respective Writings and Discoveries;

9: To constitute Tribunals inferior to the supreme Court;

10: To define and punish Piracies and Felonies committed on the high Seas, and Offences against the Law of Nations;

11: To declare War, grant Letters of Marque and Reprisal, and make Rules concerning Captures on Land and Water;

12: To raise and support Armies, but no Appropriation of Money to that Use shall be for a longer Term than two Years;

13: To provide and maintain a Navy;

14: To make Rules for the Government and Regulation of the land and naval Forces;

15: To provide for calling forth the Militia to execute the Laws of the Union, suppress Insurrections and repel Invasions;

16: To provide for organizing, arming, and disciplining, the Militia, and for governing such Part of them as may be employed in the Service of the United States, reserving to the States respectively, the Appointment of the Officers, and the Authority of training the Militia according to the discipline prescribed by Congress;

17: To exercise exclusive Legislation in all Cases whatsoever, over such District (not exceeding ten Miles square) as may, by Cession of particular States, and the Acceptance of Congress, become the Seat of the Government of the United States, and to exercise like Authority over all Places purchased by the Consent of the Legislature of the State in which the Same shall be, for the Erection of Forts, Magazines, Arsenals, dock-Yards, and other needful Buildings;—And

18: To make all Laws which shall be necessary and proper for carrying into Execution the foregoing Powers, and all other Powers vested by this Constitution in the Government of the United States, or in any Department or Officer thereof.

### Section 9
1: The Migration or Importation of such Persons as any of the States now existing shall think proper to admit, shall not be prohibited by the Congress prior to the Year one thousand eight hundred and eight, but a Tax or duty may be imposed on such Importation, not exceeding ten dollars for each Person.

2: The Privilege of the Writ of Habeas Corpus shall not be suspended, unless when in Cases of Rebellion or Invasion the public Safety may require it.

3: No Bill of Attainder or ex post facto Law shall be passed.

4: No Capitation, or other direct, Tax shall be laid, **unless in Proportion to the Census or Enumeration herein before directed to be taken.**$^Z$

5: No Tax or Duty shall be laid on Articles exported from any State.

6: No Preference shall be given by any Regulation of Commerce or Revenue to the Ports of one State over those of another: nor shall Vessels bound to, or from, one State, be obliged to enter, clear, or pay Duties in another.

7: No Money shall be drawn from the Treasury, but in Consequence of Appropriations made by Law; and a regular Statement and Account of the Receipts and Expenditures of all public Money shall be published from time to time.

8: No Title of Nobility shall be granted by the United States: And no Person holding any Office of Profit or Trust under them, shall, without the Consent of the Congress, accept of any present, Emolument, Office, or Title, of any kind whatever, from any King, Prince, or foreign State.

### Section 10

1: No State shall enter into any Treaty, Alliance, or Confederation; grant Letters of Marque and Reprisal; coin Money; emit Bills of Credit; make any Thing but gold and silver Coin a Tender in Payment of Debts; pass any Bill of Attainder, ex post facto Law, or Law impairing the Obligation of Contracts, or grant any Title of Nobility.

2: No State shall, without the Consent of the Congress, lay any Imposts or Duties on Imports or Exports, except what may be absolutely necessary for executing it's inspection

Laws: and the net Produce of all Duties and Imposts, laid by any State on Imports or Exports, shall be for the Use of the Treasury of the United States; and all such Laws shall be subject to the Revision and Control of the Congress.

3: No State shall, without the Consent of Congress, lay any Duty of Tonnage, keep Troops, or Ships of War in time of Peace, enter into any Agreement or Compact with another State, or with a foreign Power, or engage in War, unless actually invaded, or in such imminent Danger as will not admit of delay.

## Article II (Article 2 - Executive)

### Section 1

1: The executive Power shall be vested in a President of the United States of America. He shall hold his Office during the Term of four Years, and, together with the Vice President, chosen for the same Term, be elected, as follows

2: Each State shall appoint, in such Manner as the Legislature thereof may direct, a Number of Electors, equal to the whole Number of Senators and Representatives to which the State may be entitled in the Congress: but no Senator or Representative, or Person holding an Office of Trust or Profit under the United States, shall be appointed an Elector.

3: The Electors shall meet in their respective States, and vote by Ballot for two Persons, of whom one at least shall not be an Inhabitant of the same State with themselves. And they shall make a List of all the Persons voted for, and of the Number of Votes for each; which List they shall sign and certify, and transmit sealed to the Seat of the Government of the United States, directed to the President of the

Senate. The President of the Senate shall, in the Presence of the Senate and House of Representatives, open all the Certificates, and the Votes shall then be counted. The Person having the greatest Number of Votes shall be the President, if such Number be a Majority of the whole Number of Electors appointed; and if there be more than one who have such Majority, and have an equal Number of Votes, then the House of Representatives shall immediately chose by Ballot one of them for President; and if no Person have a Majority, then from the five highest on the List the said House shall in like Manner chose the President. But in choosing the President, the Votes shall be taken by States, the Representation from each State having one Vote; A quorum for this Purpose shall consist of a Member or Members from two thirds of the States, and a Majority of all the States shall be necessary to a Choice. In every Case, after the Choice of the President, the Person having the greatest Number of Votes of the Electors shall be the Vice President. But if there should remain two or more who have equal Votes, the Senate shall choose from them by Ballot the Vice President.

4: The Congress may determine the Time of choosing the Electors, and the Day on which they shall give their Votes; which Day shall be the same throughout the United States.

5: No Person except a natural born Citizen, or a Citizen of the United States, at the time of the Adoption of this Constitution, shall be eligible to the Office of President; neither shall any Person be eligible to that Office who shall not have attained to the Age of thirty five Years, and been fourteen Years a Resident within the United States.

6: In Case of the Removal of the President from Office, or of his Death, Resignation, or Inability to discharge the Powers and Duties of the said Office, the Same shall devolve on the

Vice President, and the Congress may by Law provide for the Case of Removal, Death, Resignation or Inability, both of the President and Vice President, declaring what Officer shall then act as President, and such Officer shall act accordingly, until the Disability be removed, or a President shall be elected.

7: The President shall, at stated Times, receive for his Services, a Compensation, which shall neither be increased nor diminished during the Period for which he shall have been elected, and he shall not receive within that Period any other Emolument from the United States, or any of them.

8: Before he enter on the Execution of his Office, he shall take the following Oath or Affirmation:—"I do solemnly swear (or affirm) that I will faithfully execute the Office of President of the United States, and will to the best of my Ability, preserve, protect and defend the Constitution of the United States."

## Section 2

1: The President shall be Commander in Chief of the Army and Navy of the United States, and of the Militia of the several States, when called into the actual Service of the United States; he may require the Opinion, in writing, of the principal Officer in each of the executive Departments, upon any Subject relating to the Duties of their respective Offices, and he shall have Power to grant Reprieves and Pardons for Offences against the United States, except in Cases of Impeachment.

2: He shall have Power, by and with the Advice and Consent of the Senate, to make Treaties, provided two thirds of the Senators present concur; and he shall nominate, and by and with the Advice and Consent of the Senate, shall appoint

Ambassadors, other public Ministers and Consuls, Judges of the supreme Court, and all other Officers of the United States, whose Appointments are not herein otherwise provided for, and which shall be established by Law: but the Congress may by Law vest the Appointment of such inferior Officers, as they think proper, in the President alone, in the Courts of Law, or in the Heads of Departments.

3: The President shall have Power to fill up all Vacancies that may happen during the Recess of the Senate, by granting Commissions which shall expire at the End of their next Session.

### Section 3

He shall from time to time give to the Congress Information of the State of the Union, and recommend to their Consideration such Measures as he shall judge necessary and expedient; he may, on extraordinary Occasions, convene both Houses, or either of them, and in Case of Disagreement between them, with Respect to the Time of Adjournment, he may adjourn them to such Time as he shall think proper; he shall receive Ambassadors and other public Ministers; he shall take Care that the Laws be faithfully executed, and shall Commission all the Officers of the United States.

### Section 4

The President, Vice President and all civil Officers of the United States, shall be removed from Office on Impeachment for, and Conviction of, Treason, Bribery, or other high Crimes and Misdemeanors.

## Article III (Article 3 - Judicial)

### Section 1

The judicial Power of the United States shall be vested in one supreme Court, and in such inferior Courts as the Congress may from time to time ordain and establish. The Judges, both of the supreme and inferior Courts, shall hold their Offices during good behavior, and shall, at stated Times, receive for their Services, a Compensation, which shall not be diminished during their Continuance in Office.

### Section 2

1: The judicial Power shall extend to all Cases, in Law and Equity, arising under this Constitution, the Laws of the United States, and Treaties made, or which shall be made, under their Authority;—to all Cases affecting Ambassadors, other public Ministers and Consuls;—to all Cases of admiralty and maritime Jurisdiction;—to Controversies to which the United States shall be a Party;—to Controversies between two or more States;—**between a State and Citizens of another State;** —between Citizens of different States, —between Citizens of the same State claiming Lands under Grants of different States, and between a State, or the Citizens thereof, and foreign States, Citizens or Subjects.

2: In all Cases affecting Ambassadors, other public Ministers and Consuls, and those in which a State shall be Party, the Supreme Court shall have original Jurisdiction. In all the other Cases before mentioned, the Supreme Court shall have appellate Jurisdiction, both as to Law and Fact, with such Exceptions, and under such Regulations as the Congress shall make.

3: The Trial of all Crimes, except in Cases of Impeachment, shall be by Jury; and such Trial shall be held in the State where the said Crimes shall have been committed; but when not committed within any State, the Trial shall be at such Place or Places as the Congress may by Law have directed.

### Section 3

1: Treason against the United States shall consist only in levying War against them, or in adhering to their Enemies, giving them Aid and Comfort. No Person shall be convicted of Treason unless on the Testimony of two Witnesses to the same overt Act, or on Confession in open Court.

2: The Congress shall have Power to declare the Punishment of Treason, but no Attainder of Treason shall work Corruption of Blood, or Forfeiture except during the Life of the Person attainted.

## **Article IV** (Article 4 - States' Relations)

### Section 1

Full Faith and Credit shall be given in each State to the public Acts, Records, and judicial Proceedings of every other State. And the Congress may by general Laws prescribe the Manner in which such Acts, Records and Proceedings shall be proved, and the Effect thereof.

### Section 2

1: The Citizens of each State shall be entitled to all Privileges and Immunities of Citizens in the several States.

2: A Person charged in any State with Treason, Felony, or other Crime, who shall flee from Justice, and be found in another State, shall on Demand of the executive Authority of the State from which he fled, be delivered up, to be removed to the State having Jurisdiction of the Crime.

3: No Person held to Service or Labor in one State, under the Laws thereof, escaping into another, shall, in Consequence of any Law or Regulation therein, be discharged from such Service or Labor, but shall be delivered up on Claim of the Party to whom such Service or Labor may be due.

## Section 3

1: New States may be admitted by the Congress into this Union; but no new State shall be formed or erected within the Jurisdiction of any other State; nor any State be formed by the Junction of two or more States, or Parts of States, without the Consent of the Legislatures of the States concerned as well as of the Congress.

2: The Congress shall have Power to dispose of and make all needful Rules and Regulations respecting the Territory or other Property belonging to the United States; and nothing in this Constitution shall be so construed as to Prejudice any Claims of the United States, or of any particular State.

## Section 4

The United States shall guarantee to every State in this Union a Republican Form of Government, and shall protect each of them against Invasion; and on Application of the Legislature, or of the Executive (when the Legislature cannot be convened) against domestic Violence.

**Article V** (Article 5 - Mode of Amendment)

The Congress, whenever two thirds of both Houses shall deem it necessary, shall propose **Amendments** to this Constitution, or, on the Application of the Legislatures of two thirds of the several States, shall call a Convention for proposing Amendments, which, in either Case, shall be

valid to all Intents and Purposes, as Part of this Constitution, when ratified by the Legislatures of three fourths of the several States, or by Conventions in three fourths thereof, as the one or the other Mode of Ratification may be proposed by the Congress; Provided that no Amendment which may be made prior to the Year One thousand eight hundred and eight shall in any Manner affect the first and fourth Clauses in the Ninth Section of the first Article; and that no State, without its Consent, shall be deprived of its equal Suffrage in the Senate.

## Article VI (Article 6 -
### Prior Debts, National Supremacy, Oaths of Office)

1: All Debts contracted and Engagements entered into, before the Adoption of this Constitution, shall be as valid against the United States under this Constitution, as under the Confederation.

2: This Constitution, and the Laws of the United States which shall be made in Pursuance thereof; and all Treaties made, or which shall be made, under the Authority of the United States, shall be the supreme Law of the Land; and the Judges in every State shall be bound thereby, any Thing in the Constitution or Laws of any State to the Contrary notwithstanding.

3: The Senators and Representatives before mentioned, and the Members of the several State Legislatures, and all executive and judicial Officers, both of the United States and of the several States, shall be bound by Oath or Affirmation, to support this Constitution; but no religious Test shall ever be required as a Qualification to any Office or public Trust under the United States.

**Article VII** (Article 7 - Ratification)
The Ratification of the Conventions of nine States shall be sufficient for the Establishment of this Constitution between the States so ratifying the same.

### The Bill of Rights

**Article [I]** (Amendment 1 - Freedom of expression and religion) [13]
Congress shall make no law respecting an establishment of religion, or prohibiting the free exercise thereof; or abridging the freedom of speech, or of the press; or the right of the people peaceably to assemble, and to petition the Government for aredress of grievances.

**Article [II]** (Amendment 2 - Bearing Arms)
A well-regulated26 Militia, being necessary to the security of a free State, the right of the people to keep and bear Arms, shall not be infringed.

**Article [III]** (Amendment 3 - Quartering Soldiers)
No Soldier shall, in time of peace be quartered in any house, without the consent of the Owner, nor in time of war, but in a manner to be prescribed by law.

**Article [IV]** (Amendment 4 - Search and Seizure)
The right of the people to be secure in their persons, houses, papers, and effects, against unreasonable searches and seizures, shall not be violated, and no Warrants shall issue, but upon probable cause, supported by Oath or affirmation, and particularly describing the place to be searched, and the persons or things to be seized.

**Article [V]** (Amendment 5 - Rights of Persons)
No person shall be held to answer for a capital, or otherwise infamous crime, unless on a presentment

or indictment of a Grand Jury, except in cases arising in the land or naval forces, or in the Militia, when in actual service in time of War or public danger; nor shall any person be subject for the same offence to be twice put in jeopardy of life or limb; nor shall be compelled in any criminal case to be a witness against himself, nor be deprived of life, liberty, or property, without due process of law; nor shall private property be taken for public use, without just compensation.

### Article [VI] (Amendment 6 -
### Rights of Accused in Criminal Prosecutions)

In all criminal prosecutions, the accused shall enjoy the right to a speedy and public trial, by an impartial jury of the State and district wherein the crime shall have been committed, which district shall have been previously ascertained by law, and to be informed of the nature and cause of the accusation; to be confronted with the witnesses against him; to have compulsory process for obtaining witnesses in his favor, and to have the Assistance of Counsel for his defense.

### Article [VII] (Amendment 7 - Civil Trials)

In Suits at common law, where the value in controversy shall exceed twenty dollars, the right of trial by jury shall be preserved, and no fact tried by a jury, shall be otherwise re-examined in any Court of the United States, than according to the rules of the common law.

### Article [VIII] (Amendment 8 - Further Guarantees in Criminal Cases)

Excessive bail shall not be required, nor excessive fines imposed, nor cruel and unusual punishments inflicted.

**Article [IX]** (Amendment 9 - Unenumerated Rights)
The enumeration in the **Constitution**, of certain rights, shall not be construed to deny or disparage others retained by the people.

**Article [X]** (Amendment 10 - Reserved Powers)
The powers not delegated to the United States by the Constitution, nor prohibited by it to the States, are reserved to the States respectively, or to the people.

## *FOREWORD*

Our country has changed; we are no longer the bastion of freedom we once were. Somewhere along the line our beloved nation has taken a hard turn left and we have been steadily driving down a road towards totalitarianism. The general public seems to be completely oblivious to it, and those who have noticed are struggling to get others to wake up.

Everything is backwards; patriots and war veterans are now the terrorists, Islamic radicals are our allies, and it is considered racist to believe that minorities can be successful without government welfare. We are over eighteen trillion dollars in debt, an amount that can never be paid back, and we are told we are in a recovery. Our president shows absolutely no regard for our Constitution or the rule of law, and we are made to believe that we oppose him out of a deep-rooted sense of racism.

We are truly on the verge of the "fundamental transformation" promised by President Barack Hussein Obama, only, it is safe to say that many had no idea what the term "fundamental transformation" meant.

Many people wonder how it is we have reached this point. How did America, the land where "this would never happen here," succumb to the tyranny we now face? This is not an easy question to answer. There are many variables; however, it is safe to say that this has been a long, tedious process, and slowly but surely we have been conditioned to accept it through education and propaganda. In my opinion, this isn't even a good enough answer because to condition people to accept their enslavement means to completely rewire their natural sense of what is right and wrong. In this book I intend to show you that this is exactly what is occurring in our educational system.

I didn't write this book in order to get down to the very last detail of every aspect of this agenda. Rather, I wrote it in order to correlate events we see playing out on the world stage with the actual material I was being taught in college. I wrote the book to share with you my personal experience of learning how this agenda is being implemented and what I was learning in school that motivated me to research exactly what was going on. I am convinced beyond any reasonable doubt that our education system has been set up in order to indoctrinate our population into the tenets of Communism/Socialism so we will be unable to resist a complete takeover, wherever that may come from.

I began telling my story by writing comments under the articles of other patriotic writers. Slowly but surely I was encouraged to begin writing my own articles, and through the help of some amazing people I was being read on Freedom Outpost, Patriot Update, and The Save America Foundation. Eventually I was invited to start a website with my current writing partner, Fred DeRuvo.

It is through the articles I wrote, which mainly revolved around the use of propaganda that I developed a clear picture of what was going on. This book sums up this experience and attempts to highlight the very methods being used to "brainwash" us into compliance.

Many people may ask why there is no mention of Common Core in this book. It is my belief that Common Core represents the final version of all that came before it, and a failure to understand what led to its creation would make any discussion of it meaningless. Again, this is just my personal opinion and I certainly do not mean to suggest that Common Core is a "non-issue."

I included the text of the US Constitution because I was appalled by how many people have never read it.

*"Your children will live under Communism...*

*"You Americans are so gullible.  No, you won't accept Communism outright; but we will keep feeding you small doses of Socialism until you finally wake up and find that you already have Communism.  We won't have to fight you; we'll so weaken your economy until you fall like overripe fruit into our hands."*

*Nikita Khrushschev*
*Premier of the Soviet Union, 1958 to 1964*

# 1

# My Great Awakening

I don't really know how to start, but I know that I need to say something. You see, as we watch our nation slip further and further into the abyss of complete totalitarianism, I can't help but feel I witnessed the very process being used first hand. I spent five years being educated by "extreme left-wing ideologues" in a social work program in Tulsa, Oklahoma, and I have to say, what I witnessed explains a lot of what we are seeing happen to our country.

After serving ten years in the Marine Corps and the Army, I was dumbfounded at the blatant Anti-Americanism on display in the classes I attended. It was as if the people in my presence all shared one common value, and that was a vile hatred for America and the belief that we, as a nation, were what was wrong with the world. Even more shocking was the number of professors I had, between three different colleges, who openly admitted to being Socialists while pushing their anti-American ideals on an unsuspecting class.

The willingness with which these students accepted the false premises and lies being told to them was disheartening. The only thing that kept going through my mind was the soldiers fighting a war for freedom that nobody cared about. It wasn't long before I realized that there was an agenda at work, one that entailed blinding the eyes of the students to truth and destroying their ability to reason for themselves.

It was an agenda that entailed pushing a left-wing worldview while comparing opinions to lies and false statistics in order to sway the opinion of people whose ability to think was destroyed in high school. This agenda entailed a well thought-out plan, many decades in the making, to transform The United States of America from a nation of individual liberty, to one of bondage and servitude to the global elite. In short, I realized that I was being educated by Communists and that the nation's education system was being used as one of the main catalysts of transformation.

# 2

# Using Education to Demoralize America

*It takes from 15 to 20 years to demoralize a nation. Why that many years? Because this is the minimum number of years required to educate one generation of students in the country of your enemy exposed to the ideology of [their] enemy. In other words, Marxism-Leninism ideology is being pumped into the soft heads of at least three generations of American students without being challenged or counterbalanced by the basic values of Americanism; American patriotism.* —Yuri Bezmenov

This is a concept that is difficult for many people to understand. Why would our American universities deliberately educate people into the tenets of Communism/Socialism when America is known for its liberty and prosperity? To understand this fully you have to go all the way back to Karl Marx and Charles Darwin. Karl Marx is the founder of economic Communism and Charles Darwin, obviously, is known for his "theory of evolution."

This is not intended to be a historical lesson, but a little understanding is in order. Karl Marx believed that the state should be the main means of production in society and that all of history represented a class struggle between those that controlled production and the workers that produced the goods. In his opinion, this represented the oppressed and the oppressor. He needed a reason to explain why people should be subjugated and controlled by the state. To answer this he turned to Darwin's evolution theory. According to Darwin, man was no more special than the supposed primordial ooze from which he sprang; therefore, man should be managed and controlled like any other animal. This was the beginning (though it could really go back to the theory of dialectical materialism) of Communism.

The idea that man should be subjugated to an all-powerful state is not new by any means; however, these new explanations were, and they took off very rapidly, and the results were disastrous. You see, once God was removed from the equation there was no purpose for man, so when Communist dictators such as Vladimir Lenin and Joseph Stalin—not to mention Hitler, Pol Pot, Mao Tse Tung, Che Guevara and others—saw that people rejected their ideas, they murdered them.

All in all, throughout the twentieth century 160 million people were murdered or starved to death by Communist regimes, yet for some reason, we have Communist professors still pushing the same lies in our universities today. The lie is that capitalism is based on greed and that America is a selfish society whose economic system only favors the (white privileged) rich. The lies are that Americans are suffering under the hands of greedy capitalists while Socialist countries, such as the European Union, are enjoying the fruits of everyone's labor with "universal healthcare." The lies are that America is the main contributor to "global warming," and the only way to save the planet is to "de-regulate" our industrial-based economy—an industrial-based economy, mind you, that created the highest standard of living on the planet.

Finally, the biggest lie of all is that America is a racist nation that treats its minority populations as if they are still slaves. These are the lies currently being used in an effort to demoralize America.

# White Privilege and the Demoralization of America

**W**hat was most significant about my social work education was the subject of "white privilege." Essentially, white privilege is the concept that enables the Left to accuse the white man of being "racist" for any reason. Based on concepts like "critical race theory" and "Black Liberation Theology," white privilege education sums up American society as one that benefits the white man and the white man only.

My introduction to white privilege education entailed a professor making the subtle suggestion that any student who had family members who voted for John McCain in the 2008 election instead of Obama did so because they were racist. I couldn't believe what I was hearing because this coincided with real-world events in which Barack Obama and the Left were accusing Republicans of racism every time they disagreed with an agenda item, mainly Obamacare.

White privilege also found its way into other social work subjects like homosexual rights, where white men were referred to as the "oppressor" of gay people. Mainly, though, white privilege education was being used to drive a wedge between black and white Americans in an effort to keep racial tensions alive. The purpose is to create enough hate and discontent to organize minority communities against the alleged "white institutions." It appears to be working, too; the recent violence we have witnessed resulting from the police shooting of Michael Brown and the riots in Ferguson and Baltimore stem right from the "white privilege" ideology. Black people in America have been systematically taught to believe they are oppressed victims while being encouraged to hang on to their historical roots of slavery. One particular lesson from one of my social work classes sums this idea up nicely.

A successful black woman goes to see a social worker to try to alleviate her symptoms of depression. The social worker is white (why that matters so much I'm not sure), but the woman is black, is financially successful, and complains of depression. Based on the tenets of "critical race theory" and "Black Liberation Theology," the social worker suggests that perhaps the successful black woman' s depression is stemming from the fact that she has "lost roots to her historical oppression" and is feeling as if she may have sold herself out to the "white man's culture."

This was an actual lesson written within the covers of one of my social work textbooks. The social worker in question was actually trying to convince this woman to give up her ideas of pursuing wealth and being career orientated in favor of being a victim. This makes perfect sense when you understand the Left and their objectives. Historically speaking, it has been the Left and the Democrat party that have supported slavery and segregation. It was the Democrat party that formed the KKK as well, and not only did they hunt down blacks, they hunted down Republicans that supported them too.

This is a history that has been all but forgotten, of course. The Democrat party assumed the position of the "caretaker" of the black population when President Lyndon B. Johnson enacted the "Great Society" program that promised blacks a life "free of responsibility," as it was now the government's role to provide for them.

The truth is Johnson's predecessor, President Eisenhower, had tried to pass a civil rights bill while Johnson was still the Senate Majority Leader for the Democrat party. In much the same way that Harry Reid worked to undermine our political system's integrity, Johnson worked to keep this civil rights legislation from becoming law—that is, until he became president. Johnson took this legislation as his own and is quoted as saying, "*I'll have those ni\*\*ers voting democratic for the next two hundred years.*" The point is that he deliberately passed a bill that he knew would do little more than enslave the black population to welfare. The intent of the Democrat Party was to create a permanent voting base. They are employing a similar strategy with the massive influx of illegal immigrants being allowed to cross our border.

Regrettably, a huge portion of the black population can be counted on again and again to vote Democrat. The sad reality of their "oppression" is that it is the Democrats they vote for who have presided over the inner city ghettos for decades. It has been the Democrat party that governs the cities where blacks murder blacks in gang warfare and drugs run rampant. All these Democrat politicians have to do is throw out some epithet that blames "white Republicans" for their predicament and it's a sure win.

The unfortunate reality is that the very idea of racism has been completely redefined. I said "idea" instead of definition for a reason; the actual word "racism" was invented by Communist Revolutionary Leon Trotsky to discredit all opposition to Communism. That's a story for another time, however. Most people understand racism to be a vile hatred for a person simply because of skin color. The Democrats, through white privilege education, have drastically changed that. Racism now means believing that black people can exist and compete on an equal footing with the white man. Let me say that again. The Democrats have successfully changed the definition of racism to believing that black people are as capable as whites. The liberals in our society believe that black people need welfare in order to be able to survive in the world of "white privilege." Wouldn't that be the same as suggesting that black people aren't as good as white people? Wouldn't this mean that the Democrat Party is still the party of racism? Of course it would, but don't say that in a college classroom; you may be accused of having white privilege.

It makes sense that the Left would think this way because they are the party of Darwin and not God. Remember that the Democrat Party booed God in the 2012 Democratic National Convention, which means they side on the theory of evolution. In other words, white liberal Democrats probably do think that the white man is a higher form of "evolved human being" and therefore it makes sense that they would view the black man as "inferior" and in need of their "enlightened assistance."

The truth about America's past with slavery is being obscured and "redefined" in an effort to demoralize the nation. There is so much history that is being kept from the public that there is no way this race baiting could go on if people knew the truth. For example, many people don't realize that white Europeans, known as the Slavs, were the first slaves to land on the shores of the New World. Many people have been led to believe that it was the British who ran the slave

trade, when in fact the Arabs had been running slaves from Africa for many centuries before America was even discovered.[1] Even to this day, while liberals in America play the race card, millions of blacks are still enslaved in Muslim countries around the world. A common theme you hear from college professors is that the Constitution was written to support the institution of slavery, and they often misquote the misunderstood "three-fifths compromise" to prove this point.

*White Privilege, White Slave*

Most of this white privilege education stems from the history of black slavery and black oppression throughout the eighteenth, nineteenth and early twentieth century's. In fact, I have written many articles detailing the facts about the Democrat Party's involvement in suppressing civil rights legislation, creating the Ku Klux Klan, and implementing Jim Crow segregation laws, after decades of successful integration, no less. I could go further by pointing out that Woodrow Wilson, known for being America's first Fascist president, was the one responsible for re-segregating what had already been desegregated. The unfortunate reality here is that we have all been told lies concerning slavery in America. I am not suggesting that blacks were not slaves—they were—however, they were viewed by the slave owners as more valuable than the other slaves. The other slaves who arrived on American shores nearly a century before any African slaves that is, the white slaves from Eastern Europe.

The word "slave" actually originates from the word Slav, which is a term that was used to describe whites from Eastern Europe. Do you think that the professors at our public universities, who are trying to convince your children to believe in critical race theory, will ever teach them that?

While history typically teaches us that black slaves were beaten, chained, murdered and raped by their evil white slave masters, it

---

[1] http://histclo.com/act/work/slave/ast/afr/afr-ea.html (01/08/15)

turns out that white slaves were enjoying some of these same privileges long before the black slaves arrived, even as early as the sixteenth century. In fact, nearly half of all first arrivals to American shores were white Europeans.

It was not uncommon for half of the slaves loaded onto the boats for the journey across the seas to be dead by the time they arrived because of the horrible conditions they endured. These conditions were equivalent to, if not worse than, those of the African slaves in later years. Whites who were born into slavery were forced into becoming slaves just the same as blacks, and they remained enslaved for the duration of their entire lifespan, even when blacks were able to purchase their freedom. It was not uncommon to see black slave owners, and it was not uncommon to see free black men owning white slaves. In fact, America's first slave owner was a black man, and by 1830 over 3,775 black families owned black slaves. These are just a few examples of what is missing from our history books.[2]

Many of these white slaves were also brought over from Australia, which, of course, was an exile location of sorts for Britain's criminals. The Waltham Act of 1723 brought nearly one hundred thousand white slaves from Australia to American shores. Even before the voyage to the New World the poor working class of England often found themselves and their children being kidnapped and sold into slavery. In fact, the origins of the word "kidnap" date back to these times.

Historically speaking, these white slaves were generally referred to as indentured servants. If any academic discussion arises about white slaves they are sure to be referred to in this manner. The term indentured servant only serves to minimize the fact that white Europeans were America's first slaves, and they were treated just as horribly as, if not worse than, the black slaves.

---

[2] http://topconservativenews.com/2012/03/americas-first-slave-owner-was-a-black-(man/ (01/08/15)

*The Three-Fifths Compromise and the Incremental Abolishment of Slavery*

Just like the subject of white privilege itself, this section on the three-fifths compromise was motivated by an actual experience in which a college professor used it to suggest America is racist. While not fully understanding her point at the time, the accusation of my country being "racist" coinciding with America's first black president was enough to spark my curiosity and force me to research it for myself. This is what I learned by actually studying the Constitution, something that, sadly, not enough young people are interested in doing because of their leftist indoctrination.

The truth about the Constitution and how it pertains to the issue of slavery is quite different indeed than the idea the radical Left wishes to foster in our young people. While our founding fathers may have been slave owners, they were also men of conscience. It was the writing of the Constitution itself that actually paved the way for the abolishment of slavery. The founding fathers knew that a nation founded on freedom would not be able to maintain such an institution. In some ways you could argue that the abolishing of slavery is akin to the one-hundred-year plan of the Communists to change our culture. The founding fathers knew that abolishing slavery would be no easy feat, but they took incremental steps in doing so nonetheless.

One of these incremental methods written into the Constitution itself is the three-fifths compromise. Ever a favorite clause of the leftists, it is one often used to spark a reaction from unsuspecting students. Imagine, if you will, listening to a lectured about the institution of slavery, and a professor callously proclaims that the founders only viewed blacks as being three-fifths of a person. This was a strategy that one of my professors used, and it is extremely successful. It is easy to use, of course, because these students generally know nothing about the Constitution or the subject of "apportionment for representation." This pertains to how many representatives a state may have based on its population. Do you see where this is going?

The three-fifths compromise was levied against the southern slave-owning states as a "collective" method of counting the slaves. The "three-fifths" meant that the slaves were only counted as three-fifths of their population in order to limit the number of representatives the slave-owning states could send to the Congress, thus limiting the influence the slave states had in the legislature. The founding fathers also did something that forced the slave-owner states into an attitude of impartiality towards the institution itself. This provided "conflicting interests," if you will, that eventually aided in the abolition of slavery. They applied the same "three-fifths" rule as a means of determining the South's tax liability, which was based on representation. These measures together were anti-slavery provisions in the Constitution that worked to lessen the influence of slave states and the incentive to keep slavery alive as an institution (*The Heritage Guide to the Constitution*, p. 54).

While many in education are pushing the idea that the Constitution was written to protect slavery, and that the three-fifths compromise was a racist clause written to subjugate Africans, the truth is clearly the opposite. The writing of the Constitution paved the way for the freeing of the slaves and the abolishment of the institution from American shores. How many nations, at the time the Thirteenth Amendment was ratified, still maintained legal forms of slavery? Many nations to this day still do. In fact, the United States was one of the first to make slavery illegal, and that is what our young people should be taught. If you are a young student tired of your leftist professors' delusional diatribes, throw this at them next time they say the founding fathers were racists.

*My Own White Privilege*
It was my own personal experience with this "white privilege" concept that put me on the metaphorical warpath with the Left. As I

mentioned earlier, I was majoring in the field of social work because I truly had a desire to help the less fortunate. Never in my wildest dreams would I have ever expected to be taught that the only under-privileged people in America were black. Nor did I ever expect to be told I wasn't fit to be a "professional helper" because of my right-wing leanings, but that is exactly what happened.

You see, I truly felt as if I were fighting for my country against a re-lentless enemy that was hell-bent on the fundamental transformation promised by Barack Obama. Virtually everything that came out of my professors' mouths was a lie or distortion of the truth spoken to sway people's hearts and minds to the Left. Maybe I was driven by a sense of guilt, knowing I was released from the military on a medical dis-charge and didn't deploy to the warzone, or maybe I felt the gullible liberals in my class needed to see someone passionately defend America. Either way, the lies were not going to go unchallenged, not on my watch.

The professors hated me. They hated my military tee shirts and the conservative manner in which I conducted myself. They hated that I could challenge them on almost any issue, but what they hated the most was that I understood how to be a good counselor. I understood how to connect with people, and because I was a right-winger who rejected the ideas of white privilege or social justice, I was somebody who simply could not be allowed in the field of social work. At the time, of course, I was unaware of social work's connection to Social-ism/Communism; however, I was about to become very interested in researching it.

At the end of the first semester of my bachelor's program, I was called into my adviser's office, where I was expecting to simply be told how I did during the semester and what my strong and weak points were. I suspected that my challenging attitude was irritating my professors, but I never expected this. I was explicitly told that I was not fit for the field of social work because I didn't believe in "social justice." Then, as if that wasn't enough, another professor came in and cited my rejection of white privilege as another reason for being unfit for the field. This was unbelievable to me, and my blood was boiling. My adviser went on to explain that she was the gatekeeper of the profession and it was up to her to ensure that people who don't share social work values are not admitted into the field. She explained that all social workers were Left-leaning, and if I was offended by white privilege I wouldn't like the program because the whole curriculum revolved around it. So there it is, proof from the horse's mouth of an agenda to inundate American students with the lie that all white people are racist.

At this point I wasn't going to allow them to tell me what I could or could not major in. I accused them of discriminating against me because I'm a conservative and a disabled veteran. I actually challenged the false assumption of having "white privilege" while being discriminated against for disagreeing with white privilege. With that being said, they suggested that a meeting be set up with the department chair, between all of us. I reluctantly agreed; however, I cut them off at the pass and attended the meeting with the department chair on my own terms, where I showed up with a lengthy letter addressed to my congressman. I was ultimately allowed to stay in the program but I was no longer interested in helping the unfortunate; I wanted to know what the heck was going on.

What I eventually learned was that conservatives in social work programs across the country were experiencing the same type of discrimination. The National Association of Scholars had published a report entitled *The Scandal of Social Work Education,* which highlighted several instances of this. In one case, a student filling an internship requirement in a local congressman's office was kicked out of the program for writing a welfare reform proposal that was "not liberal." This further demonstrates proof of an attempt to indoctrinate people into left-wing thinking.

It isn't just social work education where there is an extreme liberal bias. The entire "higher education system" has been taken over by liberals who are attempting to portray the false science of evolution as the truth. Christian students generally find themselves at odds with the curriculum and, when voicing their opinions, find themselves at the receiving end of harsh, discriminatory treatment from liberal professors.

With all of this being said, it became self-evident that social work education was the catalyst for pushing an extreme left-wing agenda with the ultimate goal of transforming America into a Socialist state.

# 4

# The Purpose

Hopefully by now you are beginning to see America in a different light than the one portrayed by the Left. You may be asking yourself why they would be teaching such lies. As mentioned before, the purpose is to demoralize the nation. While there are many other issues that have served the same goal, we have focused on the issue of racism because that is the primary tool currently being employed by the Left. The purpose is to cause as much chaos and confusion as possible so the end goal of Communism/Socialism will be more acceptable in your eyes. You see, the

one thing the Left fears is your understanding of truth; if you have the ability to reason, to see through the fog and come to logical conclusions, you are a threat to the Left. If you can discern a lie from the truth you will find yourself the target of vicious attacks designed to discredit and humiliate you because the Left fears the truth, and because they fear truth, it must be destroyed.

Just as is the case with white privilege, the destruction of truth is being employed in our nation's public school systems with concepts like "moral relativism" and educational techniques such as "values clarification" or "emotional virtue" education. The end goal is to cause enough confusion in the minds of our younger generations that they have no clue which leg they stand on, nor do they have any idea how to defend anything they may have once believed in. This process is called ideological subversion. Take it from the words of former KGB operative, Yuri Bezmenov.

> *In reality, the main emphasis of the KGB is not in the area of intelligence at all. According to my opinion and [the] opinion of many defectors of my caliber, only about 15% of time, money, and manpower [are] spent on espionage as such. The other 85% is a slow process, which we call either 'ideological subversion,' or 'active measures'—in the language of the KGB—or 'psychological warfare.' What it basically means is, to change the perception of reality of every American to such an extent that despite the abundance of information, no one is able to come to sensible conclusions in the interests of defending themselves, their families, their community and their country. —Yuri Bezmenov*

There is no doubt that modern-day America is strife with chaos and uncertainty. Most people just go about their daily lives without giving any second thought to what's going on around them. If asked to clarify their thoughts on any one issue, many Americans will find themselves stumbling over their responses, not knowing what to say, or they will simply spout off the latest talking points. Sadly, this applies to people on the Right and the Left. The reason for this is that the idea of truth has been destroyed in our society. Even in the classroom students are taught to view only the professor's position as truth and everyone else's as "biased opinion." This is accomplished by the skillful employment of "peer reviewed" journals, which students are limited to while doing research. The only thing they are ever exposed to is liberal opinion.

One of the most effective methods used to destroy truth in any society is the teaching of "moral relativism."

Moral relativism is defined as:

> The philosophized notion that right and wrong are not absolute values, but are personalized according to the individual and his or her own circumstances, or cultural orientation. It can be used positively to affect change in the law (i.e. promoting tolerance for other customs or lifestyles) or negatively as a means to justify wrong doing or law breaking. The opposite of moral relativism is moral absolutism, which espouses a fundamental, natural law of constant values and rules, and judges all people equally irrespective of individual circumstances or cultural differences.[3]

A society that has no "absolute value" on which to stand is one that will fail. The purpose of bringing moral relativism into our education system is to completely destroy our ability to search for an "absolute truth" in any subject. If a student is taught to believe that all religions, for example, are the same, and there isn't one that espouses any superior virtue, he is less likely to look to religion for answers and in-

---

[3] http://legal-dictionary.thefreedictionary.com/Moral+Relativism

stead looks to the state. If a student is taught that his or her particular values are not "morally different" than anyone else's, he or she is more likely to allow these values to fade when a skilled facilitator (teacher) is able to present them in a negative light.

There was a time when the United States stood solidly upon the Judeo-Christian worldview. This was destroyed in the 1950s, however, when the Communists successfully removed prayer from the public schools. Many Socialists argue that "correlation doesn't equal causation" in science. This may be true to a degree, but social science is not a real science, and it seems reasonable to conclude that the removal of prayer in school would only lead to the problems we are now facing today.

Let's face it, at that time in America's history children could buy shotguns out of the back of a comic book, without their parents' permission, and there weren't any "mass school shootings." So what happened? Social science and moral relativism replaced God, that's what happened.

Looking at current events in America today, it is easy to see where moral relativism is being used to encourage the spread of hate and discontent. Just look at the issue of race, for example; moral relativism is embedded in the ideals of "white privilege." Across the country, black on white crime is becoming an out-of-control epidemic. The skillful rhetoric of race-baiters like Al Sharpton, Eric Holder and Barack Obama are no doubt contributing to the problem; however, it is the moral relativism of their argument, and the number of times it has been pumped into the soft heads of American students, that makes it so successful.

Moral relativism is used to make black on white crime acceptable. Moral relativism, when it comes to the issue of race, justifies the hatred of the white man based on the lies discussed in the last chapter concerning slavery. In any situation in which a white man may commit a violent crime against a black, it is classified as a hate crime. Virtually every ethnic group in America is protected by some sort of hate crime legislation, meaning any crime committed by a white against a minority is automatically associated with hate and racism. If a black man attacks a white man, however, it is blamed on decades of institutional racism, and the perpetrator is generally viewed by the mainstream media as a "victim of white privilege."

Eric Holder, during his tenure as Attorney General of the United States, made it a policy not to charge minorities with hate crimes because it is impossible for them to be "racist." This is another facet of white privilege; minorities do not have the "power of the institutions" in order to be able to discriminate against the white man; therefore, they cannot be racist.

Sadly, it is the power of the institutions being exercised by the race-baiting Socialists in charge that are responsible for the black man's current predicament. The race baiting and encouraging of violence is all based on lies and Socialist agendas; it is doing nothing but turning people who could have done something with their lives into cop killers and criminals. It is the continuation of the "oppressed victim mentality" that has destroyed the black family and individual initiative in the black community. Once again, I argue that it is the Democrat Party responsible for the very institutional racism they claim to be fighting against.

Moral relativism can be seen in many other aspects of our society as well. Essentially, when you remove the idea of there being a "moral absolute," anything becomes acceptable, even the most repulsive acts.

*Moral Relativism and Multiculturalism*
My first experience with moral relativism was actually in a class called "Positive Psychology," as opposed to a social work class. Psychology, like social work, is primarily made up of leftists and is in fact

a field of work developed by the Communists. I will get into more of that later; for now, however, I want to discuss a book called the *Happiness Hypothesis*.[4]

The class was required to read this book, and I have to tell you, I was absolutely shocked by its content. Basing the whole context of the book on the idea that there is no absolute moral value, and that the values people have are all constructed on their own "opinions" or cultural outlooks, the author goes on to give some pretty heinous examples. The most disturbing was the idea that incest is only morally wrong because people choose for it to be so, and that there is no "absolute universal value" that governs human sexuality. When you combine this dangerous idea with other liberal concepts such as "multiculturalism," you are paving a road which allows absolute evil to dominate.

Multiculturalism is the idea that some things that are not acceptable in our culture are not necessarily wrong and need to be viewed from another aspect because they may be perfectly acceptable in another culture. The most recent example that can be given here is the tyrannical culture of Islamic Sharia Law and its push into the west.

It is perfectly acceptable in the culture of the radical jihadist to murder those who slander their god. It is acceptable to stone women and lie to push the cause of Islam. In America, or the Christian culture, all of these are absolute in the sense that they are wrong; however, with the push of a "multicultural society" based on the tenets of moral relativism, we are expected to tolerate the intolerable. To suggest that an Islamic terror attack is actually a "terrorist attack" has become racist and insensitive. We are supposed to view these deplorable acts with compassion and an understanding that it is America's fault.

---

[4] http://happinesshypothesis.com/(01/11/15)

In the United States we have recently seen attempts to push Sharia Law into our court systems. In Oklahoma, for example, a move to put Sharia Law in Oklahoma courts was put on the ballot in the 2010 elections; however, it was voted down by an overwhelming majority. In other cases we have actually seen Muslims accused of raping their spouses use the Sharia culture as a defense in American courts, because Islam refuses women the right to refuse sex. In one such case the judge sided with the Muslim because of "cultural sensitivities."[5]

In another case, an American judge sided with a Muslim after he attacked an atheist for wearing a Muhammad costume. It is culturally "OK" for a Muslim to attack someone if he is offended by those mocking his religion.[6]

*Child Sexual Abuse*
The most frightening aspect of the multicultural, moral relativism paradigm is the belief that all cultures, all people can live side by side in complete peace and harmony with no objections to each other's "cultural norms." There are some things, as demonstrated in the last section concerning Islam and Sharia Law, which are simply intolerable. Child sexual abuse is one of those things.

Yet under the guise of multiculturalism, there is a tireless minority within the "oppressed" homosexual community that is trying to repeal the age of consent laws concerning the appropriate age at which a child can engage in sexual intercourse. If they are successful in doing this, having sex with a child may be the next protected civil right, as they are claiming they are culturally oppressed by age of consent laws. In fact, there are certain groups who claim that adult males having sex with male children is "beneficial" and provides the young

---

[5] http://pamelageller.com/2010/07/sharia-islamic-law-in-new-jersey-court-muslim-husband-rapes-beats-sexually-abuses-wife-judge-sees-no.html/ (01/11/15)
[6] http://www.christianpost.com/news/pa-judge-accused-of-using-sharia-law-to-defend-muslim-who-attacked-atheist-70455/ (01/11/15)

boy a nourishing relationship. The following is taken from a research paper I did as a student at The University of Oklahoma.

> *There is an effort by age of consent advocates to have the term "child sexual abuse" defined in different ways. They are suggesting that the term should only be used if the child has experienced some negative outcome from the encounter[7] or did not engage freely in the act.[8] Otherwise, sex between adults and children should be considered just that, adult-child sex and not abuse.[9]*

> *Furthermore, [psychologist Dr. Bruce] Rind and his colleagues suggest that the term child sexual abuse not be used at all when dealing with adolescent children because they are more likely to be interested in sex and should be free to choose their own sexual partner. They also point to the idea that sex between adults and children has been frequent throughout many cultures and should not be considered un-normal human sexual behavior. This goes along with the earlier stated idea that today's societal norms are out of date and irrelevant.*

> *Bruce Rind and his colleagues seem to think that sexual abuse is not harmful to the child at all; or rather, only if they are already predisposed to having emotional problems because of some other familial issues, or if they have determined that they were not participating freely. In other words, Bruce Rind and his associates are suggesting that adolescent children freely engaging in sexual activity with adults can yield more positive results if*

---

[7] Rind, B., Bauserman, R., & Tromovitch, P., (1998) A Meta analytical examination of assumed properties of child sexual abuse using college samples. Psychological bulletin 124(1) 22-53
[8] Rind, B., Bauserman, R., & Tromovitch, P., (1998) A Meta analytical examination of assumed properties of child sexual abuse using college samples. Psychological bulletin 124(1) 22-53
[9] Ibid

*the child is educated on sex and engages in this behavior of his own free will. These findings are being published by prominent organizations such as the American Psychological Association. It should be noted that the research conducted by Rind and associates was used for a legal argument for the legalization of sex with children.*[10]

*This move to legalize sex with children has got to be stopped somehow because if not, it is only a matter of time before sex with children is legalized for the purpose of recognizing what one group of people consider to be their "human right."*

I included all this information as a means of demonstrating the dangers multiculturalism and moral relativism represent to society. If mankind can be brought to believe that there is no universal right or wrong which governs us all, then there are virtually no limits to the evils that can overtake us, because almost anything can be justified.

My own experience with this in the classroom comes from not only having a lesbian professor, but also from being forced to watch a movie portraying Harvey Milk as a civil rights hero. For those who may not know, Harvey Milk was California's first gay man elected to a city council position. The truth about Harvey Milk is that he was a child molester, who as an adult male engaged in sexual relationships with young boys.

In the field of social work education, gays in America are represented as one of the *oppressed* classes, and the white man is classified as their oppressor. This concept is known as "heterosexual privilege." Just as is the case with white privilege theology, heterosexual privilege depicts regular, everyday couples as being bigots because of their "privileged status" in society. At the time I was living in a neighborhood that had a lot of gay people in it, and they all owned homes

---

[10] Sorotzkin, B., (2002) The denial of child abuse: The Rind et, al controversy. Journal of psycho history - - www.narth.com/docs/denial.html

and vehicles and they had jobs too. One couple owned a beauty salon. I would refer to these facts every time gays were presented as "oppressed victims." I was told that this wasn't enough and nothing would suffice until total equality was achieved.

It is safe to say, as we watch the battle for same-sex marriage rights being waged, that the issue of homosexual rights is being used as another means of demoralizing America. (The case for gay marriage had made its way to the Supreme Court of the United States while I was finishing this book.)

# 5

## The Struggle to Define Social Change

**T**hus far we have discussed three of the main pillars being used to transform our nation. White privilege, moral relativism and multiculturalism are being pushed in our universities as a means of bringing about "social change" by portraying America as a racist, oppressive nation.

It's interesting, because while pursuing the degree I kept hearing the words "social change" over and over again. In many ways it was nothing more than a "catch phrase" that students would use to impress the professor. There were so many times when someone would "accentuate" the phrase to bring it some special emphasis, as if to prove their idea had merit and needed to be implemented for the sake of "social change." I was very curious; I understood what type of change they wanted, but I wasn't sure they understood what they were trying to change. In class I would ask them in front of everybody, just to see what response I would get. I would then recite some part of the Bill of Rights, in an effort to teach them what rights they already have under the Constitution, and describe what the consequences would be if the change they sought came to be. Yes, I really did this in the classroom, and it would make a lot of people angry because they had no leg to stand on and could offer no competitive argument. (I challenged many other positions taken by my professors as well, which I will discuss in later chapters.) What they generally resorted to was acting offended and upset because I was allegedly wasting their learning time. No one seemed to care, however, when time was wasted agreeing with the professor. Such is the way, I suppose.

It seemed that the more the semesters progressed, the more and more I was convinced that people were deliberately being "dumbed down" in a very systematic manner. During the "white privilege" portion of the first semester, for example, I watched the entire class give a presentation explaining how they had never realized they were so "privileged" as white people and how they had never understood the extent to which their actions and attitudes revolved around racism. I was truly dumbfounded; especially when I saw everyone's reaction as I stood in front of the class and said being white doesn't make me a racist. I was bound and determined to hold my ground in an environment that was becoming increasingly hostile to me and my conservative beliefs. I believed these kids were being indoctrinated and that this indoctrination was somehow related to the election of Barack Obama. I decided that I was going to stand and challenge any lies being told about my country. In order to do this I had to know what games they were playing; I needed to know how they were making people believe these lies so I could effectively counterbalance them.

# Critical Thinking or Critical Theory?

I n the meeting I mentioned in an earlier chapter, the one with the chair of the social work department, I was asked by her if I thought of myself as a "critical thinker." Not completely sure what critical thinking meant I answered yes. You see, most people would argue that the problem with American education is that students are not being taught to be "critical thinkers." This thinking is false, because truthfully, people do not know what critical thinking is. It seems logical to assume that critical thinking would entail thinking with "urgency," or thinking for the purpose of coming up with the best possible solution to a problem; it is critical, or of vital importance, for example. This is not the purpose of critical thinking.

My response to the chair of the department entailed my comparison of healthcare in America to healthcare in Europe. Obamacare was a hot topic at this time, and one that sparked many not-so-intellectual debates. I thought I was demonstrating a set of "critical thinking" skills and was hoping she would see my point. She didn't; in fact, I gained nothing but a disapproving glare. This is when I realized anything but an absolute agreement with Socialism wasn't going to cut it.

The comparison I gave would be better defined, in my opinion, as analytical thinking because I was dealing with facts. Critical thinking is quite a different beast altogether. In fact, critical thinking has very little to do with thinking at all and has more to do with simply "criticizing."

Developed by German social engineers in the Frankfurt School of Social Research,[11] critical thinking is based on "critical theory," which was designed to do nothing more than bring Cultural Marxism into the United States. This is the definition of critical theory according to the Encyclopedia of Philosophy:

> Critical theory provides a specific interpretation of Marxist philosophy and reinterprets some of its central economic and political notions such as commidification, reification, fetishization and critique of mass culture.

The way it works is relatively simple. In fact, you may argue that it is a practical application of the Hegelian Dialectic, which is the problem, reaction, solution strategy. The very people who want to institute change cause the problem, which then sparks a reaction in which people demand the change they have been taught would solve the

---

[11] http://www.iep.utm.edu/frankfur/ (1/17/15)

problem. As far as critical thinking goes, students in our universities are being provided a very biased opinion of life in the United States and being encouraged to think "critically" of it (to criticize) while the professors offer up some lies on the effectiveness of Socialism as the solution to the problems. All of the major issues we now face were on the table: healthcare, gun control, racism, "corporate greed." If I only had a penny for all the times I heard the words "corporate greed" while in school.

You see, it all goes way back to the elementary years, when Marxists have their first opportunity to mold our children. If a person is brought up to believe certain things, it is very difficult to convince him otherwise. Marxists in America have gone to great lengths, and have been very successful, mind you, to control education. So when a young, impressionable college student reads in a textbook that healthcare in Europe is free and provided by the government, instead of questioning the validity of such a claim, he or she instead resorts to "criticism of American culture" and wonders why it isn't free in America. Thus, the Left has just created the rallying cry for socialized medicine.

I witnessed this first hand in social work education. The problem, however, is that there was nothing being presented to give the opportunity for the student to develop any so-called "critical thinking" skills. The material being presented offered no real statistical analysis of European socialized medicine. It did, however, make several references to the greedy insurance companies and the supposed millions of Americans who suffer needlessly because of a lack of health insurance. This is essentially how it is done. In essence, American universities are now going to great lengths to discredit capitalism and promote Socialism, and the illusion of critical thinking is another vehicle by which it is being accomplished.

I made the mistake of believing that people would want to hear the truth in an effort to prevent the disaster that is Obamacare from becoming law, but this wasn't the case. In fact, the more I tried to cite actual statistics concerning socialized medicine, the more I was discredited and targeted for humiliation. People simply didn't want to hear the truth. Even today, with the admission by Obamacare author Jonathan Gruber on January 18, 2015 that the Affordable CARE Act depended on the "stupidity of the American voter" to pass, many people still refuse to acknowledge the failure of it. Again, this is because of the way people are being trained. For far too long Americans have been taught that capitalism is evil, and we are at the point at which there is no amount of truth that will reverse their thinking.

# 7

## The Delphi Technique

So I am now beginning to understand why everyone appears to be unable to come up with an independent thought, and is willing to just go along without questioning anything. What I fail to understand, however, is how the professors are able to keep everyone from seeing any of my points as valid and worthy of consideration. This is when my own studies led to the discovery of the "Delphi Technique:"[12]

> *A systematic forecasting method that involves structured*
> *interaction among a group of experts on a subject. The*

---

[12] http://www.vlrc.org/articles/110.html (1/18/15)

*Delphi Technique typically includes at least two rounds of experts answering questions and giving justification for their answers, providing the opportunity between rounds for changes and revisions. The multiple rounds, which are stopped after a pre-defined criterion is reached, enable the group of experts to arrive at a consensus forecast on the subject being discussed.*[13]

The Delphi Technique is a method of mental manipulation that, for all practical purposes, appears to be the general format of all college classrooms today. How many times, as a student, have you been asked to participate in group discussions where you were to solve some type of social problem? That happens quite often, but what most students don't realize is that the solution of the problem has already been pre-determined, and the job of the professor is to ensure the class is brought into agreement with this solution.

It would be better at this point if we stopped thinking of professors as people who want to educate you, but rather as "facilitators," given a job to push you towards compliance with Socialism. This is exactly what they are doing with the Delphi Technique.

During your experience with group discussions you may have noticed that either the facilitator or perhaps a helper was paying close attention to the discussions. His or her job is to identify who may be making a legitimate argument against the pre-determined solution and then discredit and humiliate that person when it is time to "open up the discussion." This is done to accomplish two objectives: first, to sway any other dissenting opinions in favor of compliance; and second, to show those who cannot be brought into line what will happen to them if they don't keep their mouths shut.

---

[13] http://www.businessdictionary.com/definition/Delphi-technique.html#ixzz3PC9GUdtX (1/18/15)

This technique was actually developed by The Rand Corporation for use during the Cold War. The people involved in facilitating these discussions are highly trained "change agents" who have the ability to portray others as aggressive, hostile, or even make their arguments seem ridiculous in their disagreement with the general consensus. (Think of all the ways conservatives were portrayed for disagreeing with Obamacare.) They do this by winning favor with the audience and presenting themselves as compassionate and sympathetic to others in the room. This is how conservatism has come to be demonized—by accusing us of being "uncompassionate."

It's safe to say that this technique is so effective that it is being used in the halls of Congress. Many Americans are watching in utter disbelief while people we elect to put a stop to President Obama's Socialist agenda refuse to stand on principle. This is because the application of the Delphi Technique has been so successful, in all aspects of its use, in portraying the conservative movement as racist and uncompassionate in its objection to socialized medicine.

One of my professors was extremely successful in employing this technique. From the very beginning of the program he laid the groundwork for gaining the favor of the students by telling lies. You see, in this program we kept the same main professors the majority of the time. This was done on purpose, I would argue, so they could maintain their influence. This particular professor, a man from South Korea (also the man responsible for teaching white privilege and multiculturalism, mind you), told story after story of how horribly he was treated by white racists while attending college in the United States. One day, he even had to eat out of a trash can. His life was miserable until some kind, compassionate person gave him the money he needed to survive.

The students ate this up. No one even bothered to ask how he was able to afford college in the United States but not afford a meal. You see, this professor's position is proof of the rabid Anti-Americanism being pushed. He attended college on the taxpayer dime, which means he absolutely *had* the means to feed himself because the US government is not going to allow a foreign student being paid to go to college to starve. We all know this, but he had to prepare the minds of the students to accept the premises of white privilege and multiculturalism, so he carried out the work of a good change agent and lied his butt off. This professor later admitted to me, in so many words, that he was a Communist.

# 8

# Saul Alinsky, Occupy Wall Street, and My Fellow Student Radicals

As the social work curriculum moved along we began to focus more and more on community organizing. I really had no idea what this was, though I knew Obama was a community organizer. I can't tell you how odd the timing of all this struck me because as we began to discuss this topic, the Occupy Wall Street movement was just getting under way. Here we had thousands of kids literally begging the government for Socialism. Some of the students in my class actually did a little rabble-rousing themselves and gave a rally hoping to whip up support for the "Occupy Tulsa" protest, which, thankfully, never took off. It's funny; I remember a student coming under pressure from the university because the social work program funded a house for him to use as a "rally point," if you will. He decided to live there off the funds provided by the program. Such is the way, I suppose.

I was still a little fuzzy about how all of this fit together, but I knew there was something to it. Then it happened: we were introduced to Saul Alinsky. I never really knew who Saul Alinsky was, other than the fact that he had a "method" that was taught by Obama and that he fit somewhere on Glenn Beck's chalkboard. Well, I knew that he had a book that he had dedicated to Lucifer as well. I remember having a discussion with a young black woman who obviously admired Obama. She had mentioned that we were going to be learning about Saul Alinsky and she suggested that because of my political tenacity, I might like him. I directed her to the only website I knew of at the time that displayed his "dedication." She was a very devout Christian, so I was hoping I would at least motivate her to open her eyes a bit. I don't know if she ever did. For those of you who may not know about Saul Alinsky and his dedication to the Devil, here it is:

> *Lest we forget at least an over the shoulder acknowledgement to the very first radical; from all our legends, mythology, and history (and who is to know where mythology leaves off and history begins—or which is which) the first radical known to man who rebelled against the establishment and did it so effectively, that he at least won his own kingdom—Lucifer. —Saul Alinsky, Rules for Radicals*

If you know anything about Christianity, then you know the Devil is all about turning everything upside down. Saul Alinsky's *Rules for Radicals* is the instruction manual on how to do it.

Before I get into great detail about what I've learned about Saul Alinsky and how it ties in with what we are witnessing, I have a story to tell you. Once again, an actual college learning experience opened my eyes to the ways of the Left and what they are all about. Some of this may seem like it's a bit ridiculous, but it's the truth nonetheless.

As I have mentioned before, I was putting a lot of pressure on my professors. I was challenging every anti-American statement that came out of their mouth. I was a lone wolf with no allies. A couple of people may have sympathized with my positions, but they were not going to stand and say it. Anyway, upon hearing that the next several weeks were going to revolve around community organizing, and knowing Saul Alinsky was part of the program, I went and bought the book *Rules for Radicals*. This is where it got really fun.

After reading through it and having a crystal clear vision of what is going on in my country, I drove to the college with the book, marched up to my professor's office, and tossed it on his desk while he was sitting there. The look on his face was priceless. I asked him if he had ever read it and he told me no. I asked him if he knew it was dedicated to the Devil; he played me for a fool and told me no, and I half-heartedly believed him. As the semester progressed and we had discussions about Alinsky, I would literally quote from the book in an effort to show the students who this man was and what he was about. Sadly, the students in social work education are so far indoctrinated into Communist thought they saw nothing wrong with Alinsky's methods.

My reciting of facts and display of patriotism was starting to annoy a lot of people. In fact, I was literally told by this particular professor that I *"wasn't supposed to know about Saul Alinsky"* and I needed to keep my mouth shut. I'm not kidding, America. He really said this to me. That's not the worst of it. I was about to learn just how well those versed in the Alinsky method can take advantage of any situation.

One Monday morning, a day on which one of our eight-page research papers were due, a woman came storming into class cursing and swearing at the professor—I mean in a very abrupt, uncontrollable manner. Apparently he had told her that he wasn't going to tolerate another late paper from her and he was prepared to knock off ten points if she didn't turn it in by the deadline. This, of course, in the mind of a liberal, is a perfectly good reason to throw a temper tantrum. It is a much better option than just exercising some personal responsibility you know.

Anyhow, I was a little perturbed to say the least, and everyone in the class seemed to think this was "OK" and she had a right to be angry. If only for the simple reason that she seemed to be unable to take responsibility for her own actions, I defended the professor and told her that she had no right to be cursing and swearing. Before I knew it she was cursing and swearing at me. I moved out into the hallway and she followed in tow, calling me every name in the book and disturbing the other classes in session.

Even though my actions were in defense of the professor (yes, the same professor mentioned throughout the book), I was called to a meeting at the student affairs office because the woman who threw a fit filed a complaint against me because I "offended her." No joke—typical liberal mentality. To be fair to the school, her conduct got her kicked out; however, I am still surprised that I was called to student affairs.

I tried to talk to my professor about this but he was disinterested. It was as if he cared not one bit that I was defending him. That's what you get when you're dealing with yellow-bellied Commies, I suppose. My response to his silence was to send a letter to the president of the college. That got a response. So now I am in a meeting once again with the chair of the social work department and my professor.

They did absolutely nothing. I couldn't believe that I was sitting there and they were acting as if I had started the argument. There was one thing that the department chair had said that I didn't quite under-

stand. She said that I should be more concerned about how people *perceive* me. She didn't explain herself, but that is a typical liberal attitude. They are far more concerned with "feelings" or perceptions than with reality—well, because their feelings are the only ones that matter, of course. I was about to find out what she meant.

I went to my student affairs meeting and I have to tell you, they weren't very concerned with the incident at hand. I explained it away with relative ease. Actually, everything that came up, to the credit of student affairs, was easily explainable and proved my classmates to be nothing but liars. Two female students had sent emails to student affairs claiming they felt threatened by my presence and that I had actually threatened one of them because I told her I knew where she lived. One of them claimed that I approached her in her truck while she was getting ready to leave and that it made her uncomfortable.

What she didn't include in her email, however, was the part where I asked her, and she agreed (though later recanted), to write a letter on my behalf stating she didn't see me intentionally start the original argument that started this whole mess. The other woman failed to mention that I knew where she lived because she had asked me where I live. When I told her, she told me she lived nearby on a particular street; upon hearing the name of the street and remembering what car she drives, I was able to determine where she lived because it is right next to a neighborhood Wal-Mart. In other words, this conversation took place between four or five people who were all discussing what part of town we were from.

The explanations I gave above are the very same ones I gave to student affairs. No action was taken aside from an "unofficial academic probation" that didn't go on my record. It was almost as if someone was simply telling me to keep my mouth shut. Well, it didn't work; my professor got an earful from me and I accused him of allowing the students to pull Alinsky tactics on me. You see, the department chair and my professor both knew what those emails said, they both knew that I wasn't a threat to anyone, and while they may not have orchestrated the situation on purpose, they were sure willing to see if it could play to their advantage. In essence, they employed "rule number eight" from Alinsky's *Rules for Radicals*:

> *Keep the pressure on, with different tactics and actions, and utilize all events of the period for your purpose.*

So now there is absolutely no doubt as to what type of people I am surrounded by and what the agenda is. This is a complete breakdown of the moral and cultural standards of the American citizen. The teaching of Alinsky tactics is to justify the notion that the ends justify the means. You see, it didn't matter how they got rid of me, as long as they did it. They knew that they had no grounds to do so, so by allowing these fallacious emails to be sent, they were hoping nature would take its course.

This is where I really began to understand what Communism and Socialism was all about. It started making a lot more sense as my professor began talking about "creating a utopia" and seeking total equality.

You see, Communists believe they can create a perfect world where everyone is exactly the same. I tried explaining to fellow students that total equality meant the equality of having nothing; however, they had been so inundated with Communist propaganda that they were willing to suffer that so long as everyone was equally poor. In their minds, this was a superior system as opposed to one in which individuals were able to succeed based on the efforts of their own merits. As far as Alinsky is concerned, his method taught that the highest level of morality entailed sacrificing your own morality for the ultimate objective of creating this perfect world. Liberals are 100 percent committed to the objective. They are all ready and willing to play their little part if they believe it will advance the agenda. This is what Alinsky had to say:

*To say that corrupt means corrupt the ends is to believe*
*in the immaculate conception of ends and principles.*
—*Saul Alinsky, Rules for Radicals*

This is the essence of moral relativism. There is no universal right or wrong, no absolute moral standard except for what liberals deem to be so. The hypocrisy is staggering because the creation of a Socialist "utopia" is their moral absolute. The very notion that there is no right or wrong can't exist without a basis for a universal absolute; in other words, they claim that there is no truth other than the one they want you to believe, and that is that there is no truth. Ludicrous, isn't it?

*Social Justice, Occupy Wall Street and "Tax the Rich"*
Another major aspect of social work education is the premise that students must be on board with the idea of "wealth redistribution." This is called social justice, and it is the motivating factor behind any left-wing political agenda. The very same professor who told me I was "unfit for social work" because of my opposition to white privilege also stated that the whole program revolved around social justice. The general attitude is that the rich should be taxed to give to the poor, because the capitalist system in which we live is inherently unfair and biased against minorities.

As I mentioned before, the Occupy Wall Street protests were occurring at the time and it baffled me how easily people in my class were persuaded by such a movement. What I saw in this movement was a bunch of spoiled kids, with degrees in fields that offered nothing to society, angry about having to pay back college loans, throwing a temper tantrum. Yet they were held up on a pedestal as a shining example of how to protest the system. I thought it was disgusting, and in class discussions I often times would mention the nasty messes being left behind by these protestors and the fact that they were defecating on police cars. I would point out the fact that these "wannabe Communists" were vandalizing privately owned businesses while simultaneously driving paying customers from local stores. My fellow classmates, on the other hand, thought they were "true revolutionaries," fighting for social justice and "total equality." I can't tell you how many times I heard "the rich need to pay their fair share" from some kid who probably never worked a day in his life.

At this point in time, I was literally driving myself insane arguing with idiots. There was nothing that could be said to these folks to make them see the fallacy of their Socialist indoctrination. The irony was right in front of their face, yet they refused to see it. You see, while they were being indoctrinated into the "social justice" ideology, their president, Barack Obama, was doing the very same thing they were so angry at Republicans for doing. He was favoring big corporations and allowing them to get away with "not paying their fair share."

Jeffrey Immelt, president of General Electric, served as President Obama's Jobs Czar in 2010. He was tasked with lowering America's unemployment rate. Despite being assigned such a monumental task, Immelt was creating more jobs in China than at home.[14]

If this wasn't bad enough, he also did so without having to pay any taxes.[15] So while the Obama-ites were chanting "tax the rich, tax the rich," Obama himself was actually helping his billionaire buddies profit big time. It was as if these students had an "intellectual inability" to look at these facts and analyze them on any level whatsoever. This might be a good time to remind you of the goal of brainwashing, or "ideological subversion," which will be discussed in greater detail later.

---

[14] http://theeconomiccollapseblog.com/archives/ge-ceo-jeffrey-immelt-the-head-of-obamas-jobs-council-is-moving-jobs-and-economic-infrastructure-to-china-at-a-blistering-pace (1/20/15)
[15] . http://hotair.com/archives/2011/03/25/obamas-favorite-ceo-gets-ge-out-from-paying-any-us-taxes/ (1/20/15)

*In reality, the main emphasis of the KGB is not in the area of intelligence at all. According to my opinion and [the] opinion of many defectors of my caliber, only about 15% of time, money, and manpower [are] spent on espionage as such. The other 85% is a slow process, which we call either 'ideological subversion,' or 'active measures'—in the language of the KGB—or 'psychological warfare.' What it basically means is, to change the perception of reality of every American to such an extent that despite the abundance of information, no one is able to come to sensible conclusions in the interests of defending themselves, their families, their community and their country"—Yuri Bezmenov*

Not only was President Obama letting Jeffrey Immelt and GE get away with not paying taxes, he was wasting billions of taxpayer dollars on failed solar energy companies. He was essentially letting the CEOs of these companies pocket the taxpayer subsidies when the company went belly up.

In other words, President Obama is just as much a friend to large corporations as any Republican ever was. The difference with the Democrat party is the fact that they have the media and educational establishment ready and willing to blindfold the sheep. This is why nobody seems to care that President Obama's own personal wealth has increased from $1,300,000 *before* running for president to $11,473,336 in 2011 *after* he took office. This is an over 700 percent increase. It's OK in the minds of liberals because he is compassionate and earns his money by caring for the oppressed.[16]

Another example that highlights this well is "Obamacare" and the insurance companies. Americans wanting free healthcare never stopped to think twice about how much the "evil insurance compa-

---

[16] http://www.snopes.com/politics/obama/networth.asp (1/22/15)

nies" would profit when individuals were forced to buy a healthcare plan. This law, like everything else Obama does, takes money from the working class and redistributes it to the rich, and because they have been conditioned to believe that Socialism is compassionate, they never stop to think about what's really going on.

Look folks, it's a fact that people's premiums increased when the law was passed.[17]

It's also a fact that many insurance companies helped write the law.[18] If these two facts aren't enough to make you wonder why anyone would support this unconstitutional legislation, then perhaps you should wonder why Congress has exempted themselves from the law. Anyway, I digress. The main point is that Obama has everyone convinced he is for the little guy; however, his actions and policies are supporting the rich he convinces you to hate.

With all of this being said, what we essentially have is a young generation that has been "dumbed" down to the point of not knowing which leg to stand on when it comes to any issue. The most they can do is "go along to get along," which is what they were taught in elementary education. (I'll discuss this more in a later chapter.)

The Occupy Wall Street Crowd, as far as I could tell, were mindlessly begging for a social system they knew nothing about, because their college professor told them it would be more fair. You could show these people, as well as my college classmates, the cold hard facts of Socialism and it didn't matter; the indoctrination took over. In my opinion, this was proof of Yuri Bezmenov's contention that you could provide a generation with so much "disinformation" that they would never know what to believe.

---

[17] http://benswann.com/premiums-skyrocket-198-congress-exempts-themselves-from-obamacare-provisions/ (1/20/15)

[18] http://www.nhteapartycoalition.org/tea/2013/08/06/insurance-companies-helped-write-obamacare/ (1/20/15)

At this point I was 100 percent convinced of a conspiracy to condition people to accept Communism. The teaching of Saul Alinsky, moral relativism, multiculturalism and the brainwashing methods of the Delphi Technique were all coming together nicely. Truthfully, it is the only explanation that makes any sense, and when you consider the real objectives of President Obama's original profession, community organizing, it should all come together nicely for you too.

The very premise of organizing is to amass political power to affect "social change," and those who get the power will do anything to retain that power once it is established. One of the tactics used is called Institutional Deviance, and its purpose is downright evil:

> *To destroy the structure of apathy, by stirring up dissatisfaction and discontent; disrupting existing complacent expectations and breaking down the individualistic orientations of community residents. —Practice Of Macro Social Work*

In other words, the community organizer is literally trained in the art of telling lies and working off the emotions of the people. Tell people they are oppressed and they will surely follow any plans to alleviate their oppression. If you have been following closely you should be able to see that this entire program is one big exercise in community organizing. The whole premise of social work itself is to keep minority populations in a state of discontent (this will be discussed in greater detail later) so they can be easily organized to put pressure on the system that is allegedly oppressing them. As I mentioned in the chapter on white privilege, they are literally teaching minorities that white people are their oppressors.

To understand this further we are going back to Alinsky. In *Rules for Radicals* he quotes Fyodor Dostoevsky, a Russian scholar and Socialist who wrote the following:

*Any revolutionary change must first be preceded by a passive, affirmative, non-challenging attitude toward change among the mass of our people. They must feel so frustrated, so defeated, so lost, so futureless in the prevailing system that they are willing to let go of the past and chance the future.*

This is my favorite quote from Saul Alinsky's book for a couple of reasons. First, it describes perfectly the motivations behind our educational system and the false narrative they tell about America. Second, it also explains, in my opinion, the gutless, cowardice actions of the GOP when it comes to standing up to the Democrats. The idea is to destroy the morale of the population to the point that they have no idea what to believe and will be ready and willing to accept whatever is offered in its place. In other words, the Republicans are willing accomplices.

This is why the textbooks portray Socialism as a superior system. This is why the Congress acts helpless in the face of Obama's power grabs; they are aiding the Democrats in creating the illusion that the system is broken and must be reformed. Finally, this is the only explanation as to why you have generations of people who are supposedly educated willing to ditch the US Constitution in favor of Socialism/Communism.

# Cloward and Piven

Just like Saul Alinsky, Richard Cloward and Frances Fox Piven are names that many of us learned from Glenn Beck's "chalkboard" on his former Fox news show. Despite this, I once again can tie their influence into my own college experience. Richard Cloward is actually deceased; however, his wife (Piven) is alive and well, teaching in the social work department at Columbia University.

What is significant about this? Not only did President Obama attend Columbia University, I have had several professors who have admitted to having "Socialist leanings" who earned their PhD in social work from Columbia. It would be safe to assume, then, that at some point they fell under the influence of Piven. This is disturbing because Piven has direct ties to Communists and is responsible for organizing voter registration schemes; she even had her hands in the "Occupy Wall Street" protests (more on this later). Perhaps what this Socialist duo is best known for is their plan to implement Socialism in the United States.

*The "Wait" Of the Poor*
In the 1966 issue of "The Nation" magazine, Richard Cloward and his wife, Frances Fox Piven, published their plan to bring Socialism to the United States. In an article entitled "The Weight of the Poor: A Strategy to end Poverty,"[19] Cloward and Piven argue for the creation of an unsustainable welfare state in which everyone is eligible for some kind of benefit from the federal government. They do this knowing full well that such a plan would overwhelm the existing welfare system, thus destroying the economy and forcing the government to implement Socialism. This plan is based on the "chaos theory" that Socialists seem to love so much. Looking at the current state of the economy, it's safe to say that this plan is well on its way to succeeding.

*The Unsustainable State of Welfare*
Even though many professors denied it, everything in social work revolved around welfare. It was all connected to social justice, the idea that wealth should be redistributed from the rich to the poor and that certain people in society were "entitled." Many people in the field of social work believe it is unfair to require people to work in order to receive welfare, and many others have no idea where welfare funds come from.

The big initiative being pushed right now, which stems directly from the Cloward-Piven strategy, is the idea that everyone in America is

---

[19] http://www.thenation.com/article/weight-poor-strategy-end-poverty# (1/22/15)

entitled to a "basic guaranteed income."[20] The claim is that this income will provide all people with their basic needs when there is no work available; however, it fails to describe exactly where this money will be coming from. This was a concept that I brought up many times in "social justice" discussions, and I'm telling you, people either don't get it, or they believe that a certain portion of the population should be forced to pay everybody else's bills.  I would argue that if fewer and fewer people were working, or being "dis-incentivized" to work through a basic guaranteed income, the government would be unable to collect the necessary funds to pay everyone this income, or any welfare, for that matter—unless, of course, we continue to borrow money from Communist China. Sadly, many of my classmates had absolutely no problem with this concept.

The students I attended class with, based on my observations, had no clue about the potential consequences of a "basic guaranteed income" because their minds have been so programmed to hate the free market. They didn't understand that wealth was created through the initiative of people willing to do the work and willing to risk their own property and prosperity. To them, everyone should be the same, and the rewards of hard work equated to nothing more than an "oppressive meritocracy," because some people succeeding more than others based on their own merits and individual initiative was unfair. In essence, they were already good little Communists.

Another concept that seemed to escape my classmates was the cost of administering the welfare state. Since the war on poverty began in 1964, The United States has spent a staggering twenty-two trillion dollars on welfare, and the poverty rate remains the same today as it was when this began over fifty years ago.[21] Those on the Left have no answer for this, though their typical response is to immediately de-

[20] http://www.usbig.net/whatisbig.php (1/25/15)
[21] http://www.heritage.org/research/reports/2014/09/the-war-on-poverty-after-50-years (1/25/15)

mand more government spending. The answer to this dilemma is relatively simple, and believe it or not, those controlling things know exactly what they are doing. It is all a part of creating the "unsustainable welfare state" described in the Cloward and Piven strategy.

Can you imagine what benefit twenty-two trillion dollars would have been to the American economy over the past fifty years? The reason the poverty rate has remained unchanged is because only a percentage of this money is actually being distributed to welfare recipients; the rest is being used to fund the paychecks and healthcare plans of the employees administering the welfare state.

Writing for the Cato Institute's Policy Analysis journal,[22] Michael Tanner demonstrates just how much money is spent annually on welfare programs. As of the article's publication in 2012, there were 126 welfare programs being funded by the federal government to the tune of 668 billion dollars for 2012 alone. When you include spending by state and local governments, which equates to over 250 billion, the total number of dollars spent per year on welfare is nearly one trillion dollars.

Given the deteriorating state of the economy and the masses of people leaving the work force, this number is undoubtedly higher today. The one trillion per year figure, according to Tanner, breaks down to an estimated sixty thousand dollars per American family. This doesn't take into consideration the amount needed to pay the workers who administer it. Clearly, this is a system that is unsustainable because the worse the economy becomes, the fewer number of people there are working to pay taxes into this system. The more money taxed from the citizens and foolishly spent by government, the worse the problem becomes, and it is all being done in order to usher in Socialism.

---

[22] http://www.cato.org/sites/cato.org/files/pubs/pdf/PA694.pdf (1/25/15)

In social work education we never took any tests. I found that to be astonishing to say the least. We did, however, watch a lot of videos. One in particular that comes to mind, which has direct implications to the subject at hand, revolved around a young mother on welfare. She was black, and she was living in public housing, collecting welfare and food stamps while going to school. Now, I have no problem with any of this up to this point, to be honest, as long as she is using her benefits to better herself in order to contribute to society. This, however, was not the intended lesson. You see, the mother in question used her welfare money to get her nails and hair done because her self-esteem was "lacking," for a lack of a better term. She then went to the welfare office and asked for more money. The lesson revolved around having the right amount of empathy to understand her situation because she was a black woman suffering under the oppression of the white man's society. To be honest, I don't remember if she received more money or not, but I do know that I was considered a racist, insensitive jerk for suggesting she learn some personal responsibility.

### Piven's Lasting Influence

The Cloward and Piven plan essentially boils down to a strategy of community organizing. We see the results of this plan culminating with the racial tensions resulting from the shooting death of Michael Brown in Ferguson, Missouri and the Baltimore riots. As I have mentioned several times before, the idea revolves around teaching people they are *oppressed*, organizing a power base and encouraging the overthrow of the existing power structure.

As far as Cloward and Piven are concerned, the idea is to make as many people as possible dependent on the system, and then deliberately crash it with the intent of causing as much chaos as possible. It's like a story I heard about a flock of seagulls. The flock, normally able to search out its own school of fish, had become so used to a local fishing charter attracting their quarry that when the boat left, the seagulls forgot how to search for food themselves.

It seems that the Cloward and Piven plan may be responsible for a bit more than many realize. In his book *Radical in Chief*, Stanley Kurtz reveals just how influential Frances Fox Piven is. Apparently, she is recognized in the community organizing profession as someone who is an authority on the history of organizing during America's early Communist movements. Frances Fox Piven sat on the Executive Committee of the Democratic Socialists of America (Kurtz).

In 1983 she delivered the opening speech at a conference that Barack Obama attended. This conference was the Cooper Union Socialist Scholars Conference. Would you like to know what her speech was about? She developed the voter registration strategy which we have witnessed being executed with the recent elections of Barack Obama and presented it to her Socialist colleagues at this conference. The following is a quote from *Radical in Chief*.

> *Piven's ties to ACORN...ran deep, and this conference would provide her with an opportunity to put forward her latest innovation—a voter registration strategy designed to radicalize the Democratic Party and polarize the country along class lines. Piven's strategy would be carried out in collaboration with ACORN, Project Vote and related organizations over the ensuing decades.[23]*

That is pretty powerful, seeing as that speech was given in 1983. It describes what we are witnessing today perfectly; the country has never been so polarized. Everybody is coming to suspect that this is all orchestrated, but when you look into the profession of community organizing it all comes together.

---

[23] Radical in Chief-Barack Obama and the Untold Story of American Socialism, (2010) Stanley Kurtz , First Threshold Editions

Remember all the news about ACORN at the beginning of Obama's first term as president? Do you remember Occupy Wall Street? It seems that Frances Fox Piven not only played a role in encouraging this kind of manufactured crisis as she gave a few speeches to Occupy crowds, but she also had extensive ties to ACORN. ACORN stands for Association of Community Organizations for Reform Now. It could be theorized that Occupy Wall Street was a part of a larger plan that was originally presented back at the Socialist Scholars Conference in 1983, which our president attended.

# 10

## The Final Semester

Thus far we have discussed the various "change methods" and "philosophies of change" I witnessed while pursuing my undergrad degree in the field of social work. It has become abundantly clear that there is an agenda at work to change the worldview of our students from one that understands the virtues of individual liberty to one that favors Communism.

From white privilege to Saul Alinsky, from the Delphi Technique to Cloward and Piven, there is definitely an effort to indoctrinate America's college students into a leftist, Marxist mindset. From what I could I see, this was the only viable explanation for why so many

people were willing to see President Obama's propaganda in the light they did. It was as if the conditioning had worked and the vast majority of Americans felt nothing but disdain and outright shame for their country, and just as Alinsky said in *Rules for Radicals*, they were willing to accept anything in the place of a system they had lost all hope in. Essentially, the agenda is to demoralize Americans to the point that they feel guilt and can no longer discern truth from lies. It seems to be working perfectly.

*The Global Citizen and Agenda 21*
While it seems that I had seen the worst that my university had to offer, I would just like to say that the worst was yet to come. In fact, it was amazing the way all of it culminated at the end of the last semester; it was definitive proof of my suspicions, to say the least.

Hanging in the halls of Oklahoma's Northeastern State University Liberal Arts Department, are posters describing the students' responsibility to be good "global citizens." The term "global citizen," of course, refers to a citizen living in a world governed by one "global government," *i.e.* the New World Order. I was amazed at the number of people who were in favor of total government control, but what was more amazing was the number of people who believed a global government would best serve the need for "social justice."

You see, the efforts to discredit America have been so successful, the Left now feels comfortable coming right out in the open and admitting its agenda. It is no secret that the Left uses the issue of "global warming" to push for global government. In the colleges, the term "climate justice" is used, or it is simply related to "social justice." In fact, many on the Left like to use the term "climate debt,"[24] which is a term used to blame rich countries on problems allegedly caused by

---

[24] http://www.democracynow.org/2009/11/23/naomi_klein_on_climate_debt_why (2/1/15)

capitalist activity. They claim that we have polluted the world so badly that global warming is our fault, and we should pay.

I can't remember if it was the very last class, or one of the last, but towards the end of the semester we watched a movie depicting the perils of global warming as solely America's fault. This movie had absolutely nothing to do with social work, except from the viewpoint of "social justice," that is. The film actually claimed that the only way to alleviate poverty in the world was to hold America responsible for global warming and make us pay.

It was much like the film shown to elementary school students, "The Story of Stuff," which introduces our children's minds to the idea that we as humans "over-consume" and are destroying the planet as a result. Keeping in true form of the Communist tradition, the film compared capitalism with Communism with the intent of teaching people that Communism would be the solution to the problem. I pointed this out only to be humiliated, as usual. Ironically, two years later in 2014, the UN climate chief, Christiana Figueres, came right out and called for a global Communist government to combat global warming. In fact, she is outright calling for a reduction in global population levels. I would have never imagined.

Essentially, the global warming agenda is best summed up by understanding Agenda 21. If you are unfamiliar with Agenda 21, here is an article I wrote on the subject.

> *Agenda 21 Simplified*
> *Agenda 21 is actually another term for "sustainable development," which originated at the Earth Summit in Rio back in 1992.[25] The whole premise of Agenda 21 is based on the belief that the world's industrial powers are destroying the environment by causing "global warming," and only by radically alter-*

---

[25] http://www.un.org/geninfo/bp/enviro.html/ (2/1/15)

*ing the way we live can the planet be saved from our destructive selves. The aim is to eliminate private property rights, remove man's footprint from the rural parts of the world and herd them into the cities, control populations, and force us to live under their rule by ensuring all nations are completely disarmed. Many will balk at this; however, I intend to resort to the source of UN materials which are out there in plain sight for all to see.*

*Let's start with the recent attacks we have seen against private land ownership in the United States, more specifically, the way our cities are rezoning the land we own and exercising more and more power over it. Communism has a long history of denying people the right to own private property; in fact, the Soviet Union removed all farmers from their land and forced them into stacked apartment complexes in the name of preserving the environment and collectivism.[26] The United States Constitution guarantees the rights of individuals to own property because property ownership is the very vehicle in which private wealth is created.*

*The UN and the rest of today's Communists are attacking the rights of property ownership precisely for that reason. They believe that when individuals own property, the wealth created by doing so is used for selfish reasons that only benefit the property owner, and thus, owning property only contributes to the creation and sustainment of poverty. Let's look at an excerpt from the United Nations Conference on Human Settlements:[27]*

**Land, because of its unique nature and the crucial role it plays in human settlements, cannot be treated as an ordinary asset, controlled by individuals and subject to the**

---

[26] http://www.sodahead.com/united-states/agenda-21-equals-national-suicide/question-1896723/ (2/1/15)

[27] http://www.un-freezone.org/habitat1.shtml(2/1/15)

*pressures and inefficiencies of the market. Private land ownership is also a principal instrument of accumulation and concentration of wealth and therefore contributes to social injustice; if unchecked, it may become a major obstacle in the planning and implementation of development schemes. Social justice, urban renewal and development, the provision of decent dwellings and healthy conditions for the people can only be achieved if land is used in the interests of society as a whole.*

*Public control of land use is therefore indispensable to its protection as an asset and the achievement of the long-term objectives of human settlement policies and strategies.*

*To exercise such control effectively, public authorities require detailed knowledge of the current patterns of use and tenure of land; appropriate legislation defining the boundaries of individual rights and public interest; and suitable instruments for assessing the value of land and transferring to the community, inter alia through taxation, the unearned increment resulting from changes in use, or public investment or decision, or due to the general growth of the community.*

*The UN believes that land ownership contributes to "social injustice;" in other words, it is unfair that some people own vast amounts of land while others own little. In order to rectify this they are going to control all the land, tax you for owning it and redistribute the resources in order to achieve social equality. While many of these objectives may sound good, there is no way that a government can ensure total equality for everyone, and every time it has been tried these governments have found it necessary to murder millions in order to achieve it.*

*While on one hand they are claiming to make everything equal for all, on the other they are doing something quite different. Many people who are following this topic have come to accept that the global elite are seeking to control the world's populations. This very document, the UN Conference on Settlements, addresses this by pointing out the problems of excessive population growth.*

***World population growth-trends...indicate that numbers of mankind in the next 25 years would double, thereby more than doubling the need for food, shelter and all other requirements for life and human dignity which are at the present inadequately met...***

*If today's food requirements for a population of seven billion people are inadequately met, how will they provide for a population of fourteen billion? Well, according to Alex Newman from the New American, the UN has a plan on how to deal with the exploding population growth in Kenya.[28] They intend to inundate the women of that country with propaganda about reproductive health, abortion and family planning in an attempt to convince them of the need to have fewer children to help them meet their population objectives. Doesn't that sound like something you would hear from some of our own politicians? Could it be possible that they are attempting to use birth control and abortion as a means of population control here in the US? I think we can all speculate on the answer to that question.*

The Communists are carrying out their agenda right under our noses because they have changed the way we think and they categorize what they intend to do as fair and just.

---

[28] http://www.thenewamerican.com/world-news/africa/item/17291-un-unveils-plot-to-reduce-african-population (2/1/15)

# 11

# In the Beginning

We have reviewed the methods used at the university level to get students to accept the Communist agenda, but how are they prepared for this conditioning beforehand? As a student, I was amazed at the way my professors were "shocked" that I would offer any resistance to their authority. It was almost as if they had expected everyone to already be good little Communists. This means that this conditioning goes back to the beginning stages of a child's education, which incidentally, has been happening for many decades.

I mentioned in earlier chapters the relationship between Darwinism and Karl Marx. Marx had adopted Darwin's theory of evolution as being the "story of natural history" that best fit his "economic theory" of Communism. It would later be proven; however, that Marx's ideas of the proletariat rising against his capitalist oppressors would not pan out; therefore, another approach was needed.

Antonio Gramsci was an Italian Communist who decided that the best way to change a culture from capitalism to Communism was by incrementally infiltrating its institutions. His plan, known as the "Long March through the Institutions,"[29] entailed the slow, methodical infiltration of every aspect of American society: government, education, the church, the family—well, you get the picture. (This is not intended to be a history lesson but to simply provide the basic information needed to understand what is happening to your country.) He understood that the process would be painstakingly slow, and in fact, he expected the plan to take at least a century to complete.

Gramsci's ideas are still relevant today as we see our society being divided into different "oppressed groups." While Marx's theory revolved around the oppressed and the oppressor, Gramsci expanded on this by defining minorities, women and even criminals as different classes of oppressed people. He also expanded on Marx's theory of how a dominant group exercises control by suggesting oppressed peoples suffer from hegemony.  He referred to these people as "organic intellectuals" (Steven Yates). This is where white privilege ideology probably came from because this refers to the way a group is suppressed by being forced to live in a system designed exclusively for the dominate social group.

Do you see how influential Antonio Gramsci was in defining the way today's progressive operates? The idea was to teach these people they were being oppressed by the dominate group and encourage

---

[29] http://archive.lewrockwell.com/yates/yates24.html (2/7/15)

them to "undermine the hegemony and defect from the dominate point of view" (Steven Yates).

While today's liberals have undoubtedly gained control over much of our nation, Gramsci's plan was to originate in the universities and trickle out to the rest of society. This plan has been extremely successful and goes a long way in describing the "political correctness" we suffer from in our country today.

Antonio Gramsci was not the only influential player in the early twentieth century. As a signer of *The Humanist Manifesto*,[30] which is described as being an Americanized version of *The Communist Manifesto*, John Dewey also played an instrumental role in introducing Marxism into our school systems. Humanism works off the premise that religion is obsolete and has outlived its usefulness. Instead of looking to God, man must look to his own achievements through science to satisfy human needs and social advancements. In other words, humanism in America is responsible for the removal of God in our public schools.

Again, much of this reverts back to Darwin and Marx, and in the case of John Dewey, Darwinism provided the belief that the highest form of evolution was "continuous positive change." These are the roots of what we see in "hope and change" today, folks.

The goal was to remove society from its roots (God) and teach it that we evolve, and that because we evolve the notion of an absolute morality is absurd, thus the birth of moral relativism in America. John Dewey believed it was the job of our education system to teach students to be good global citizens ready to surrender their ambitions to the state.

Believing that "change" is the highest ideal, and that evolution is necessary to achieve change, there can be no absolutes because abso-

---

[30] http://www.christianparents.com/humanism.htm (2/8/15)

lutes do not change; they are set in stone. God is absolute and the word of God does not change, therefore the word of God is bad. John Dewey also referred to our Constitution in that manner, believing that it was not relevant because it was not meant to change. Many people remember President Obama saying that the Constitution was a hindrance to progress. He is cut from the same cloth.

As you can see, Antonio Gramsci and John Dewey played a huge role in transforming our society, and yet most people have never heard of them. It's not like your college professor is going to introduce you to this material and admit that he or she has been tasked with brain-washing you. As soon as young children enter elementary school they are bombarded with "change strategies" that go all the way back to these two. For twelve years they are inundated with anti-American, Communist propaganda to the point that they can barely formulate an original thought. Then, they are encouraged to apply for govern-ment student loans and attend college. This is how you conquer a na-tion without ever firing a shot.

Regrettably, most Americans will never be able to understand how deep all of this goes. Our entire education system has been reformed in order to indoctrinate American students into accepting a new global form of government, or "The New World Order," as it has come to be known. Charlotte Iserbyt, Department of Education whistle-blower and author of the book "The Deliberate Dumbing Down of America," highlights the events that have taken place through the legislative process that brought us to the point we are at today. Even I was shocked to see the evidence she presented, and truthfully, if people don't accept the reality of it, they will never find themselves able to make real changes because they are fighting with blindfolds on.

One of the problems facing America today is the false "Left/Right" paradigm of American politics. Liberals and Conservatives are locked in a battle over philosophical ideologies, believing that their chosen political party represents them. Don't get me wrong; many of today's liberals are so brainwashed by this godless humanism that they can't think for themselves, and many conservatives simply believe the Republicans will fix everything. The truth is that both political parties have been selling us out and pushing a Communist agenda for a long time. While it would appear that it is purely a "Democrat agenda," it is imperative you become familiar with what Charlotte Iserbyt claims to be the truth.

Ronald Reagan is known as one of America's most conservative presidents. During this tumultuous time of radical change we see many politicians and talk radio hosts referring to Reagan as a sign of hope and inspiration. According to Iserbyt, he may be the one most responsible for what we are now seeing occur in our education system. She claims that Ronald Reagan signed education agreements with the Soviet Union that enabled them to bring their teaching methods into our country. Many will be asking how this makes any sense because Reagan will always be remembered as the one who "tore down the iron curtain."

The truth is, these agreements have been being signed for decades, and in fact, Dwight Eisenhower, another conservative icon, also signed agreements with the Russians. This started back in 1958 with something called the "Reese Committee." It was agreed that taxpayer dollars from American citizens would be paid to research and implement a peaceful merging of the Soviet Union and the United States for the purpose of establishing a world government.[31]

This is one of those subjects that seem so outrageous, so improbable, that the thought of it being real will generate more ridicule than inspire actual inquiry. All I can say is that I read Iserbyt's work and it is pretty convincing. After all, it's not like we don't have millions of

---

[31] http://www.deliberatedumbingdown.com/OtherPDFs/Iserbyt_Soviets_in_class.pdf (2/8/15.)

young "useful idiots" running around begging for Communism. If you have any interest whatsoever in restoring our nation to the "constitutional republic" it was intended to be you will read Charlotte Iserbyt's *The Deliberate Dumbing Down of America*.

## Competency-Based Education

So far I have discussed several different methods such as critical theory and the Delphi Technique that are used to guide the indoctrination process. There is also something called competency-based education. This focuses more on developing certain competencies related to job skills and career development.

Most people won't see a problem with this, which is indicative of the efforts to standardize education across the board; however, I will tell you, it is alarming. Competency-based education is modeled after the old Soviet Union model of education in which the government decided what job they would train you in based on what they thought you were good at. This was highly praised by John Dewey, whose efforts can be recognized as leading American education in this direction, as well as Ronald Reagan, who signed education agreements with the Soviet Union, as I mentioned earlier.

I believe this is why the Common Core curriculum is drawing so much attention and is increasingly being referred to as a Communist system of education. It seeks to *standardize* the human being, if you will—make us all the same, which has been the goal of the Fabian Socialists for nearly 150 years.

There is an article entitled "What is Competency-Based Education?" written by one of its proponents, Dr. Robert Mendenhall. Dr. Mendenhall is apparently one of those elites who think he knows better than the rest of us concerning our education and abilities to learn. Arguing for competency-based education, he says,

*The fundamental premise of competency-based education is that we define what students should know and be able to do, and they graduate when they have demonstrated their competency. This means we have to define the competency very clearly. Getting industry input is essential to ensure we have identified relevant competencies.[32]*

That last sentence is pretty telling in that the overall goal of this effort is the creation of an obedient work force that is simply able to perform the necessary functions of a "job" as dictated by its masters. It is getting people to accept servitude, folks—period. It is training your children and mine to accept that someone else knows what is best for them.

There are several problems with competency-based education that I think are pretty relevant here. One is the removal of honest standards and the fact that letting industry define competency means there is no set standard on what actually defines competency. It is different based on whatever job training program your children may be involved in. Who decides which children are competent for which programs? Who decides, and based on what criteria, which children are demonstrating leadership competencies? This is one of those programs doomed for failure but already praised for being a great success.

To understand this further you have to realize that much of this effort is being driven by the Marxist/humanist forces that believe man, in essence, is no different than any other animal, and his actions are merely preprogrammed reactions to any given set of stimuli. Outcome- and competency-based education are both byproducts of the Skinnerian and Pavlovian methods of conditioning, in which animals were conditioned to behave in a certain way based on a system of

---

[32] http://www.huffingtonpost.com/dr-robert-mendenhall/competency-based-learning-_b_1855374.html (2/8/15)

96

reward and punishment. In the case of your children, these humanists essentially believe that values are not universal, the Judeo-Christian worldview is oppressive, and in order to peacefully transition from a world of independent, sovereign "nation states" to a world government, children would have to be "socialized" into accepting a new order. Social psychology and Socialist propaganda have played a huge role in defining what direction education would take. Let's examine the original definition of education as opposed to the "social psychologist" reformers' definition. These definitions go back to the early twentieth century when European Socialism was first making its ways to our shores.

The New Century Dictionary of the English Language, published in New York in 1927, defines education as follows:

> *The drawing out of a person's innate talents and abilities by imparting the knowledge of languages, scientific reasoning, history, literature, rhetoric, etc.—the channels through which those abilities would flourish and serve.*

This sounds like education was originally intended to create free, independent thinkers and allow them to use their own talents and merits to strive for achievement.

The definition of education was radically altered as the influences of Marxist/humanist social science became more relevant. Viewing the learning process from the narrow lens of "physiological processes," it became very dehumanizing, as people came to be viewed as simply a body and a nervous system devoid of a soul. Social psychologist Rudolph Pintner wrote in his 1934 book *An Outline of Educational Psychology* the new "revised" definition of education:

> *Learning is the result of modifiability in the paths of neural conduction. Explanations of even such forms of learning as abstraction, and generalization demand of the*

*neurons only growth, excitability, conductivity, and modi-*
*fiability. The mind is the connection-system of man; and*
*learning is the process of connecting. The situation-*
*response formula is adequate to cover learning of any*
*sort, and the really influential factors in learning are*
*readiness of the neurons, sequence in time, belongingness,*
*and satisfying consequences.*[33]

To these social scientists, mankind is nothing but a programmable animal that can be conditioned at their will. For all practical purposes, it seems the biggest agenda item is teaching children that the Constitution is racist and an inherently "unfair" system that leaves minorities behind.

The Left literally hates the Constitution. President Obama once referred to it as a document that was flawed and described too much what the government couldn't do to you, as opposed to what it must be doing on your behalf.[34] This is indicative of the Left's belief that people are generally incapable of self-governance and must have "an elite" political body governing their whole lives.

They would like you to believe that without them you couldn't possibly make the right decisions for yourself. They would like you to believe that freedom is dangerous and enables people to live unsafe and unhealthy lives. In other words, they need you to need them far more than you really do.

The Left understands the Constitution better than most people would give them credit for; at least, the professional, political Left does. They understand that liberty is dependent upon an informed populace that understands the Constitution. They also understand that it is held together by the first Ten Amendments, which is why they

---

[33] http://www.deliberatedumbingdown.com/MomsPDFs/02Chapter%2001.pdf (2/8/15)
[34] http://www.wnd.com/2008/10/79225/ (2/21/15)

work feverishly to brainwash your children against them. If they want a compliant citizenry that is merely conditioned to obey orders then the Ten Amendments must be done away with. How do you do this? You make them afraid of freedom, and you start with the Second Amendment because that's the glue that binds the rest together.

*The Culture-Changing Pop-Tart*

After the Sandy Hook Elementary School shooting, the Left took the idea of "gun control" propaganda to new heights—in many cases, ridiculously new heights. This isn't to say that there weren't some necessary precautions that should have been taken; however, they truly allowed the idea of making children afraid of guns run completely out of control.

This is when the policy of having "gun-free zones" was shown to be the insane policy it is. One man with a gun, whether it was a security guard or a staff member with a concealed carry permit, could have ended that tragedy before it started. We all know, however, that the Left will exploit any tragedy to further its agenda of control. What ensued in elementary schools the following year is a shameful example of how the Left exploits tragic situations and uses deceitful tactics to indoctrinate children into seeing things their way.

Let me start by laying some basic groundwork here, to develop a useful reference point, if you will. Most of us, if we are between the ages of forty and sixty, remember growing up around rifles and shotguns. We attended our first hunter's safety course when we were ten and always remembered to never, ever point a gun at something we didn't intend to shoot. The Second Amendment, which was never intended to be applied to hunting, is such an ingrained part of American culture it is very difficult for most adults to understand the vile hatred the Left has for guns and the lengths to which they will go to rid you of them.

The schools are currently being used to inundate your children with "anti-gun" hysteria in the hopes that they will grow up and serve as future gun-grabbing operatives. This all started in the early part of 2013 when young Josh Welch was suspended from school for allegedly biting a Pop-Tart into the shape of a gun.[35]

Even the boy was taken aback when he noticed how shocked they were over such a ridiculous thing. He wasn't even trying to make a gun—he later admitted that he was actually trying to make a mountain—yet the school, in an effort to *create* an impression that they were concerned for the safety of the children, held fast in their decision to suspend the boy. Throughout the year similar stories continued to surface in which children were suspended for bringing toy guns to school or action figures that had little "laser guns" as an accessory.

One group of children was expelled from school when the bus driver noticed they were playing with "paintball guns" in their own front yards. The insanity seemed never-ending as these stories continued to surface throughout the year. When I was a child I brought my favorite toy guns to school for show and tell for crying out loud!

Another thing that schools were doing that only seemed to fuel the hysteria was conducting active shooter drills on campus. I would compare these to the old "nuclear war" drills of the past in which students were encouraged to hide under their desks in fear of a nuclear blast. The one thing that stands out about these drills is that they revolve around reinforcing a culture of fear and conditioning the students to look to authority in a state of panic.

I happened to witness a couple of these "intruder on campus drills" myself while working as a substitute teacher, and I have to say that this is the best description I can come up with. There is nothing

---

[35] http://www.storyleak.com/school-suspends-child-biting-pop-tart-gun/ (2/22/15)

wrong with conducting "readiness drills" if the goal is to actually save lives and the children are learning in real time how to respond "calmly" in order to think logically through a stressful situation. This is not what is happening; these drills are actually creating a generation of useless kids who will not know how to do anything except look to the government in times of an emergency.

They are ensuring a generation of people will grow up so afraid of the society around them that they will be ready and willing to give up all of their rights in order for the government to keep them safe.

Not only are they trying to scare your children into hating guns, they are also taking the privilege of rewriting our Constitution in the textbooks. The fundamental premise of our Constitution is that the government's job is to secure human rights that are endowed upon us by the very virtue that we are alive. The founders believed, as do many Americans, that our rights come from God and they cannot be taken by governments of men.

This principle was the driving factor behind the American Revolution, and this is the very principle the Left seeks to destroy. In order to be able to control us, they must indoctrinate us with the belief that rights come from government and not God. This is why they have taken the liberty of rewriting the Second Amendment in Common Core textbooks across the nation. The rewritten version reads as follows:

> *The Second Amendment: The people have the right to keep and bear arms in a state militia.*[36]

Notice how they only refer to a state militia as opposed to the Amendment's actual reading. Here is the original Second Amendment:

---

[36] http://www.thenewamerican.com/culture/education/item/17991-common-core-approved-textbooks-rewrite-second-amendment (2/22/15)

*A well-regulated Militia, being necessary to the security of*
*a Free State, the right of the people to keep and bear*
*Arms, shall not be infringed.*

There is a huge difference between the ways the word "state" is being used. In the rewritten version the word "state" is being used as an absolute base of authority from which the right to bear arms is derived. In the actual Amendment, the word "state" refers to the people, the manner in which they formed their society. Again, it can't be stressed enough that the goal is to teach young people that government, not God, is to decide which rights people will or will not exercise freely.

# 12

## Mental Health and a College Internship

There is another area in which our education system has gained massive influence, and it has had severe consequences upon our young people: mental health. Our classrooms, even as early as kindergarten, have become little psych wards where teachers are at liberty to suggest your child may need Ritalin because he can't sit still.  There is a big controversy over the use of psychotropic medication and whether diseases such as ADHD or Bipolar Disorder are even real at all. As it stands now, nearly one out of seven kids are being prescribed these medications, and frighteningly enough, the reason goes right along with the rest of the agenda: dumb down the population so they will unknowingly accept more control over their lives; make them docile enough that they accept a Communistic agenda. Consider this quote from Dr. Wayne O. Evans:

> We see a developing potential for nearly a total control of human emotional status, mental functioning, and will to act.[37]

This quote is from a 1967 meeting of top psychiatrists who met in Puerto Rico to discuss the mental health agenda. Essentially, the massive prescribing of these psychotropic drugs seems to have accomplished their goal of total emotional control. Nearly one in ten adults is being prescribed these drugs, and at the rate children are being prescribed them we are well on track to being a nation that could be considered mentally ill. Consider for a moment the idea that many of these mental health disorders are simply made up, or maybe caused by bad diets or too much television.

There simply is no real test, as there is with other medical conditions, which conclusively proves a child has ADHD or Bipolar Disorder. Yet these drugs are heavily prescribed to children, and very few seem to be asking why. Doesn't anyone else find it strange that all of a sudden children are being diagnosed with Bipolar Disorder?

Unfortunately, doctors who prescribe these drugs to children receive huge payoffs from the drug companies who manufacture them. In fact, a congressional inquiry in 2009 revealed that the studies suggesting that children would benefit from the use of psychotropic drugs were severely slanted.

Dr. Joseph Biederman of Harvard University received 1.6 million dollars to provide this research to drug manufacturing companies.[38]

---

[37] http://real-agenda.com/2015/02/24/the-largest-medical-conspiracy-ever/ (03/01/15)

This is all part of the agenda to destroy liberty in America, create a docile population and instill a Socialistic/Communistic government. This book wasn't written to provide you the stone-cold facts, statistics and research; rather, it was written to describe to the reader my own personal experience in the universities and my own awakening to the agenda. When it comes to this topic there is a story to tell that comes directly from my experience in social work education.

*The Child Welfare Internship*
Upon graduating with a bachelor's degree in social work, I realized that I was in a field that was inherently hostile to everything I believed in. I also realized that a bachelor's degree in this field was useless; you needed a master's degree in order to make any decent money. I needed to make a decision. My first four years of college were paid for by the VA Vocational Rehabilitation program and switching majors to pursue another degree would prove to be too expensive.

I decided that because I still wanted to help children I would continue on the social work path, so I enrolled in the Masters of Social Work Program at the University of Oklahoma. It was a nightmare through and through. It was like everything in the bachelor's level program on steroids. The racism elements were there; in fact, this is where the story of the successful black woman (mentioned earlier in the book) and her social worker comes from.

I was also ridiculed by a professor as she attempted to portray American service men as being racist. She had fabricated a story about a group of Marines being in group therapy for PTSD and their racist attitudes towards one of their team members for being an "Arab Marine." I challenged this assertion by saying the Marines wouldn't be racist toward him for being "Arab" if they were serving in combat to-

---

[38] http://www.askgrace.ca/psychiatrist-creates-bipolar-disorder-epidemic-children-admits-receiving-16-million-drug-company-payoff/ (03/01/15)

gether, and she attempted to ridicule and discredit me. It was truly unbelievable.

Somehow, I made it through these classes with pretty good grades; even the most leftist professors couldn't deny my skills in talking with people. This made me believe that these professors could set their biases aside and judge a person by the quality of his work and not his opinions or beliefs. I was wrong; the entire time they were gossiping about me while still operating on the belief that I wasn't fit for social work because of my political positions.

My wife used to tell me to keep politics out of my schoolwork. In social work this is very difficult to do because it all revolves around a political agenda. I would imagine that you would have to be very in tune with your own political beliefs to see it. The professors certainly are, and they can spot someone on the opposite aisle almost immediately.

One of the requirements to obtain a master's degree in social work is a sixteen-week, full-time practicum, or internship. I chose to do mine at the local Oklahoma Department of Human Services Child Welfare office. There were two reasons I choose this; one, it was a paid internship and guaranteed two years of employment after graduation, and two, it put me in direct contact with the population I wanted to help.

This internship was a disaster from the beginning. The incompetence of the people working there explains the trouble the agency is always in. Oklahoma DHS was sued, and lost, for having one of the highest infant mortality rates in the nation. In other words, more children were experiencing more suffering—or dying—at the hands of foster parents than the actual parents they were removed from. It was in this internship that I saw the true failures of liberalism and the realities of the Communist agenda.

I could go on by telling stories of being called sexist and being labeled as rude. I could tell stories of outright favoritism and incompetence or of people spreading rumors about me behind my back. Instead, I will tell the story that relates directly to the mental health agenda and the use of psychotropic drugs and how this issue led to me being denied my master's degree.

Part of the practicum experience involved visiting the local psychiatric hospitals where children were placed after being removed from their parents' custody. Not all children are placed in these facilities, and some are considered to be more "high risk" than others; nonetheless, I visited many of them. The story was the same everywhere I went: children as young as six, who didn't understand why they were there, being drugged up on as many as seven different medications. None of them understood why they were given these drugs, and many of them expressed a desire to no longer have to take them. I spent a great deal of time expressing my frustration with this, and I even went so far as suggesting that we should be working to get these kids off of drugs because if we didn't we would soon be living in a nation where everyone was considered mentally ill.

You have to understand that in the field of social work and mental health treatment, teams are set up with a psychiatrist at the head of the pecking order, and no one dares to question the psychiatrist. If he says that children need drugs, everyone will scramble to comply with his orders. The psychiatrist, after all, is often the most educated in the team, and having the label of "doctor" makes his opinion, for all practical purposes, appear to be based on serious academic inquiry. As I have already demonstrated, this is not the case. The sad reality is that these kids are being set up for a lifetime of complete dependency upon the government. They are having their livelihoods ripped from them, their state of mind is being altered, and then they are being given handouts by the same government that took them from their homes to begin with. Don't get me wrong, there are certainly situations in which children need to be removed from abusive homes; however, the textbooks skew the actual statistics and redefine words to give social work students the impression that all homes need to be "inspected" in order to keep children safe.

One day, my supervisor approached me and asked if I would talk to a young man about joining the Marine Corps. The kid was sixteen years old and was living in a local boys' home. What I didn't know at the time was that this particular kid had been diagnosed with Bipolar Disorder and was prescribed about seven different medications. Unfortunately, the Marine Corps will not accept recruits who are taking psychotropic drugs, so I asked him if there was any possibility he could begin working towards getting off of the drugs. He appeared to think that was a good idea and expressed an interest in doing so. After all, I could recognize the desire the kid had to be a Marine.

I can't begin to tell you how much trouble I caused by making such a simple suggestion. In fact, I was accused of pushing my own values onto the kid and this was used as an excuse to give me a mark of incompetence on my final review. Actually, what they said is that I was pushing the idea of joining the Marine Corps on him and that I was pushing him to get off his medication. Nowhere in my evaluation did they mention the fact that they had asked me to talk to him specifically about joining the Marine Corps, nor did anyone care to listen when I told them.

This was not the only situation in which I felt like I was specifically baited or led to perform the job in the wrong way in order to ensure I wouldn't pass the course. It was as if there was nothing I could do that was right. I later came to find out, through my supervisor's own admission, no less, that the professors at the college were sharing their negative opinions of me with the people in charge of the practicum at the Child Welfare site.

Another situation revolved around another young boy who was also prescribed a ton of psychotropic medications and had a habit of going AWOL from whatever home he happened to be in. This particular situation was a bit more serious and caused actual employees to lose their jobs as well. It all started when I had finally gotten the young man on the phone after he was reported as being lost. The DHS workers had failed to do their job by not reporting his absence to the Sheriff's department.

While speaking with him in an effort to ascertain his location, he threatened to shoot me in the face with his shotgun. I calmly told him in response that I would call the police, and that was treated as if I had just threatened his life. They said I was displaying characteristics that made me unfit to be helping children because I was being too assertive. In fact, it was almost as if they were trying to correct the situations that got them sued by taking it out on me, a student.

After getting the kid back into custody they allowed him to choose his own foster home—not one approved by the state, but with one of his friends. Is it any wonder they are constantly being sued? While at this residence he attempted to rape a young girl, and of course, he had to be picked up. One of the employees, someone who had spent some time with this kid, was asked to go pick him up, in his own vehicle, and bring him back to the office. During the car ride, the kid began tearing apart his car and calling him some very derogative racial slurs.

The employee took him back to as close to the house he came from as he could and returned to the office without him. He was fired for this. My supervisor then came to me and asked if I would go pick him up. I felt that this was entirely inappropriate because I was just a student. Needless to say, however, I went to pick him up. This was twice that I was responsible for ensuring the safe return of a kid they failed to keep proper track of, and I was just a student.

These people were such low-life liars. I really don't know how they live with themselves. Three days before graduation I was given my final evaluation. I knew things were not going well but I had no idea that they would stoop this low. I specifically asked them if there was any reason I should be worried about graduation and they said to me, and I quote, *"David, if there was a problem we would be discussing it right now."* They smiled at me as if posing for a family photo while those slimy words slithered out of their mouths; however, I believed them and went about my day anticipating graduation.

You see, in this meeting they had told me that my evaluation was completed and just needed to be signed. The next day I found out this was a complete *lie.* On the very last day of the semester, the culmination of a five-year, continuous trek through school, they called me on the phone, two hours before the end of the day, and told me I would not be graduating. They had their tracks covered, too. Anybody reading that evaluation would be convinced that they were in the right and I was simply not competent enough to have a master's degree in social work. I know the truth, however, and that truth is that conservatives who do not believe in social justice will not be permitted in the field of social work, period. After all, the professors are the gatekeepers of the profession.

I had made several attempts to reach out to the faculty at the college to tell them I was having problems. They are supposed to ensure that students are being instructed properly. In fact, if a student asks to be moved they are obligated to move them. No one helped me, not at all. They didn't even follow their own procedures concerning students experiencing difficulties. I was supposed to have a level one and two review hearing before being allowed to fail. This obviously didn't happen. The plain and simple truth is that I was deliberately set up to fail because I am a non-conformist and I rocked the boat.

# 13

## The Psychopolitical Agenda

Throughout the book I have highlighted several of the nation's biggest problems and how they correlate to what I was exposed to as a student in social work education. To think that it is all "coincidental" would be foolish; after all, we have as president a man who worked in the field of community organizing and was influenced by none other than Saul Alinsky. We have examined issues of racial identity politics, white privilege, welfare, Cloward and Piven and mental health. We have touched on the methods of indoctrination at the university and elementary educational levels, and we have touched on the subject of the UN pushing for a global government. The rest of this book will be dedicated to tying the pieces together in an effort to get you to understand the real goal of psychologically disarming you. To do this we will be examining the art of psychopolitics, which is what I believe best describes the agenda in our public schools.  This definition is from the book *Brainwashing: A Synthesis of the Russian Textbook on Psychopolitics*, by Anton Berea:

> *Psychopolitics: The art and science of asserting and main-taining dominion over the thoughts and loyalties of indi-viduals, officers, bureaus and masses, and the effecting of the conquest of enemy nations through "mental healing."*

Psychopolitics is Communist in origin, and it can best be described as the fabrication of mental disease to convince an enemy nation they are in need of "mental healing." The definition says all you really need to know. It is about asserting control over a population through the use of propaganda and educational techniques that work to con-dition rather than educate. The whole idea is to discredit the belief in God and create a need for mental health practitioners trained in the implementation of psychopolitics in order to create dumbed-down little Socialists. Based on this description it may be safe to say that the United States has been under a full-blown "psychopolitical" as-sault for many years.

After prayer was outlawed from the public schools in the 1960s we began to see an increased reliance on the use of psychologists and psychiatrists to deal with normal conditions that people once turned to God to solve. To many people this sounds crazy. After all, we live in a country where we are guaranteed the right to practice religion freely by the First Amendment to the Constitution. One would be hard pressed, however, to argue that we haven't been witnessing a relentless assault on our Judeo-Christian values by the atheistic, or better yet, Communistic, Left. These attacks are proof of the "psychopolitical" agenda.

In the old Soviet Union, the labeling of dissenters as being "mentally ill" was an effective means of eliminating political opposition. This is the same approach the Left is now taking in an effort to label religious healers as insane. Not only that, they have also gone as far as labeling those who believe in the Bible as "right-wing extremists." This is described in a report published by the Department of Homeland Security in 2009, cited in the footnote below.[39]

This classification of Bible-believing people as mentally ill is best accomplished by using mental associations in an effort to compare Christianity with the evils of Islam the world has been witnessing. Through the use of moral relativism, which has been discussed in earlier chapters, it is easy to get people to discredit all religion based on the actions of radicals. This is the goal of the Communists who employ the psychopolitical method: to give the illusion that those practicing traditional Christianity are insane and their beliefs lead to hatred, intolerance and bigotry. Take this quote from Anton Berea's *Brainwashing: A Synthesis of the Russian Textbook on Psychopolitics*:

> *Insanity must be made to hound the footsteps of every priest and practitioner. His best results must be turned into jabbering insanities no matter what means we have to use. You need not care what effect you have on the public. The effect you care about is the one upon officials. You must recruit every agency of the nation marked for slaughter into a foaming hatred of religious healing. You must suborn district attorneys and judges into an insane belief as fervent as an ancient belief in God that Christian Science, or any other religious practice that might devote itself to mental healing is vicious, bad, insanity-causing, publicly hated and intolerable.* —Anton Berea, p. 59

---

[39] http://fas.org/irp/eprint/rightwing.pdf (03/08/15.)

Remember, my degree field was social work. At the master's level, social workers can give therapy. The idea here is to break man's connection with God and re-educate him into the ways of Communism. When a person goes to a therapist, a psychologist, or a counselor, he or she is seeing someone trained as a "change agent" to bring about conformity and sees man's ways as a method of healing, not God's. This is what is occurring in our public schools in America. Our textbooks, as I have suggested many times throughout this book, are full of lessons which seek to indoctrinate people into the tenets of Communism as opposed to the values this nation was founded on. To offer further proof of this conclusion, consider the following from Berea's book on page 53:

> As every chair of psychology in the United States is occupied by persons in our connection, or who can be influenced by persons in our connection, the consistent employment of such texts is guaranteed. They are given the authoritative ring, and they are carefully taught. Constant pressure in the legislatures of the United States can bring about legislation to the effect that every student attending a high school or a university must have classes in psychology.

This virtually proves that there exists a plan to destroy the values of American citizens, within the public education system, no less, and replace them with a Communistic mindset. The goal is to discredit God altogether and replace him with psychology.

# 14

## Stated Goals of the Communist Party

I remember the day I first became suspicious about the beliefs my professors held. It was before "white privilege" and everything else that had happened, when I heard my professor from Korea trying to discredit Joseph McCarthy by talking about "McCarthyism." McCarthyism, of course, refers to the belief that Senator Joe McCarthy was paranoid about a Communist infiltration into the nation's government. Judging by the state of the nation today, I would say that Joe was right.

Cleon Skousen wrote a book called *The Naked Communist* in which he highlighted forty-five stated goals of the Communist party USA. Yes, there is such a thing, and in fact they have a new constitution waiting in the shadows as we speak. [40, 41] These forty-five goals were actually entered into the congressional record in 1963, so it is safe to say that our government—both parties, incidentally—are fully aware of them. These are the forty-five goals. If you have not read them before you should be forewarned; many of these have been accomplished:

1. U.S. acceptance of coexistence as the only alternative to atomic war.

2. U.S. willingness to capitulate in preference to engaging in atomic war.

3. Develop the illusion that total disarmament [by] the United States would be a demonstration of moral strength.

4. Permit free trade between all nations regardless of Communist affiliation and regardless of whether or not items could be used for war.

5. Extension of long-term loans to Russia and Soviet satellites.

6. Provide American aid to all nations regardless of Communist domination.

7. Grant recognition of Red China. Admission of Red China to the U.N.

8. Set up East and West Germany as separate states in spite of Khrushchev's promise in 1955 to settle the German question by free elections under supervision of the U.N.

---

[40] http://www.revcom.us/socialistconstitution/SocialistConstitution-en.pdf (03/15/2015)
[41] http://rense.com/general32/americ.htm (03/15/2015)

9. Prolong the conferences to ban atomic tests because the United States has agreed to suspend tests as long as negotiations are in progress.

10. Allow all Soviet satellites individual representation in the U.N.

11. Promote the U.N. as the only hope for mankind. If its charter is rewritten, demand that it be set up as a one-world government with its own independent armed forces. (Some Communist leaders believe the world can be taken over as easily by the U.N. as by Moscow. Sometimes these two centers compete with each other as they are now doing in the Congo.)

12. Resist any attempt to outlaw the Communist Party.

13. Do away with all loyalty oaths.

14. Continue giving Russia access to the U.S. Patent Office.

15. Capture one or both of the political parties in the United States.

16. Use technical decisions of the courts to weaken basic American institutions by claiming their activities violate civil rights.

17. Get control of the schools. Use them as transmission belts for Socialism and current Communist propaganda. Soften the curriculum. Get control of teachers' associations. Put the party line in textbooks.

18. Gain control of all student newspapers.

19. Use student riots to foment public protests against programs or organizations which are under Communist attack.

20. Infiltrate the press. Get control of book-review assignments, editorial writing, policy-making positions.

21. Gain control of key positions in radio, TV, and motion pictures.

22. Continue discrediting American culture by degrading all forms of artistic expression. An American Communist cell was told to "eliminate all good sculpture from parks and buildings, substitute shapeless, awkward and meaningless forms."

23. Control art critics and directors of art museums. "Our plan is to promote ugliness, repulsive, meaningless art."

24. Eliminate all laws governing obscenity by calling them "censorship" and a violation of free speech and free press.

25. Break down cultural standards of morality, by promoting pornography and obscenity in books, magazines, motion pictures, radio, and TV.

26. Present homosexuality, degeneracy and promiscuity as "normal, natural, healthy."

27. Infiltrate the churches and replace revealed religion with "social" religion. Discredit the Bible and emphasize the need for intellectual maturity, which does not need a "religious crutch."

28. Eliminate prayer or any phase of religious expression in the schools on the ground that it violates the principle of "separation of church and state."

29. Discredit the American Constitution by calling it inadequate, old-fashioned, out of step with modern needs, a hindrance to cooperation between nations on a worldwide basis.

30. Discredit the American Founding Fathers. Present them as selfish aristocrats who had no concern for the "common man."

31. Belittle all forms of American culture and discourage the teaching of American history on the ground that it was only a minor part of the "big picture." Give more emphasis to Russian history since the Communists took over.

32. Support any Socialist movement to give centralized control over any part of the culture--education, social agencies, welfare programs, mental health clinics, etc.

33. Eliminate all laws or procedures which interfere with the operation of the Communist apparatus.

34. Eliminate the House Committee on Un-American Activities.

35. Discredit and eventually dismantle the FBI.

36. Infiltrate and gain control of more unions.

37. Infiltrate and gain control of big business.

38. Transfer some of the powers of arrest from the police to social agencies. Treat all behavioral problems as psychiatric disorders which no one but psychiatrists can understand [or treat].

39. Dominate the psychiatric profession and use mental health laws as a means of gaining coercive control over those who oppose Communist goals.

40. Discredit the family as an institution. Encourage promiscuity and easy divorce.

41. Emphasize the need to raise children away from the negative influence of parents. Attribute prejudices, mental blocks and retarding of children to suppressive influence of parents.

42. Create the impression that violence and insurrection are legitimate aspects of the American tradition; that students and special-interest groups should rise up and use ["]united force["] to solve economic, political or social problems.

43. Overthrow all colonial governments before native populations are ready for self-government.

44. Internationalize the Panama Canal.

45. Repeal the Connally reservation so the United States cannot prevent the World Court from seizing jurisdiction [over domestic problems. Give the World Court jurisdiction] over nations and individuals alike. [42]

I underlined the goals that were most easy to relate to and that had the most to do with the topics in this book. If you can't see that many of these goals have been accomplished, and many others are "in progress," then you are simply not paying attention. Many of these "goals" can be directly attributed to events that we have seen or that we are currently seeing be played out. Take goal number forty-two, for example:

42. Create the impression that violence and insurrection are legitimate aspects of the American tradition; that students and special-interest groups should rise up and use ["]united force["] to solve economic, political or social problems.

Wouldn't this apply to the Occupy Wall Street protests we witnessed during President Obama's first term? These people were led to be-

---

[42] Ibid.

lieve that they had a right to riot and destroy the property of others based on the false precepts of "wealth inequality." The same could be said for the Ferguson protestors. While they are not students, they could be described as a special interest group, and they are being "organized" to social action by those who have taught them they are oppressed.

What about goal number forty?

> 40. Discredit the family as an institution. Encourage promiscuity and easy divorce.

The nuclear family has long been understood to be the backbone of any "free society." As long as people are free to educate their own children with their own values, there is little chance a Communist agenda could ever succeed. Therefore, this creates the need to diminish the influence parents have on their children, which is the purpose of goal number forty-one:

> 41. Emphasize the need to raise children away from the negative influence of parents. Attribute prejudices, mental blocks and retarding of children to suppressive influence of parents.

As you can see, many of these goals have been accomplished or are in full swing. What about the issue of mental health discussed earlier in the book? Goals number thirty-eight and thirty-nine address this issue.

> 38. Transfer some of the powers of arrest from the police to social agencies. Treat all behavioral problems as psychiatric disorders which no one but psychiatrists can understand [or treat].

> 39. Dominate the psychiatric profession and use mental health laws as a means of gaining coercive control over those who oppose Communist goals.

America, the story is the same no matter which way you look at it. These goals either have been accomplished or are "in progress" and soon will be. They have been moved steadily along by an educational system supported by a compliant media that hides the truth from the public and promotes news that only advances the agenda. Americans have become too distracted and too "dumbed down" by an entertainment industry that keeps people distracted with nonsensical television programming and movies that turn our brains to mush.

While you work hard to send your children off to what you consider to be "good schools," the academia elite are working feverishly to turn them into "good little Socialists." It is my intent to do whatever I can to help inform the public because it isn't just my children who will be suffering if we don't work to change course. Freedom is truly just one generation away from extinction at this point, and unfortunately, it seems very few are hearing the call to defend it.

# 15

## Fighting the Good Fight

So there you have it. That is my true story of being educated by radicals in a radical world. The entire Socialist agenda wrapped up in five years of social work education explained for all to see. This nonsense continues to this day as we see universities across the nation resort to teaching "white privilege" while insisting the values America was built upon are racist. Just recently, The University of California Irvine announced they would be banning the American Flag because they claim it is a symbol of racism and oppression.

I am not the only conservative this has happened to. If you would like to read more on the subject of social work indoctrination I would urge you to read "The Scandal of Social Work Education" published by the National Association of Scholars.[43] There is one particular story of a young man doing an internship in a local politician's office. He was tasked with writing a welfare reform bill and was failed by his professor because it was not "liberal" enough. After reading this document you will see that the universities pushing out social workers are responsible for a great many of the issues we face today; after all, the profession of social work is Socialist in origin.

I spent the following year, with the help of a student association lawyer, trying to appeal this. The process kept getting put on hold and it took the duration of the entire year before I was even able to stand before a board and state my case. I barely had a chance to talk; the chair of the social work department wasted a great deal of time exaggerating her own importance and the details of her job description. After the board closed the proceedings my lawyer and I noted that we felt we did not have sufficient time to state our case; however, they didn't even blink. In their minds I was the big bad racist, sexist conservative that isn't worth the time of day.

It was being exposed to this indoctrination and the attitudes of those in academia that awakened me to the dangers we face. I have always been a Constitutionalist; however, there was a day in my younger years when I could have easily fallen for the Left's propaganda and followed suit by exclusively blaming Republicans. In many ways you could argue that this experience has forced me to open my eyes and do my own research rather than just "go along to get along."

You see, this is what they are truly working to prevent. They would just as soon see a population that has no ability to question what they are told than have to deal with people who dare question their au-

43 http://www.nas.org/articles/The_Scandal_of_Social_Work_Education (03/01/15)

thority. They believe that they exist on a higher level than the rest of us because of the academic stature and their "degrees." They view themselves as being specifically qualified to rule because they are smarter than the rest of us; therefore, what we are truly witnessing is the establishment of a global society governed by science and the "academic elite" as opposed to common sense and natural law.

I have spent the past couple of years, after my bout with the University of Oklahoma, writing articles for "patriotic" websites in an effort to not only share my experience but to interpret world events based on my understanding of my experience. In other words, it was my exposure to Alinsky and white privilege indoctrination that enabled me to look past the headlines and understand the motives of a government that for all practical purposes seems hell-bent on our destruction. I don't mean to brag here, but events like the Ferguson riots were all too easy to predict when the whole educational system is dedicated to preserving racial bigotry.

We have a tremendous task ahead of us, America. We either begin now by taking charge of what our children are learning in school by teaching them the truth ourselves or else we will suffer the consequences. We had better learn to stand up and do what is necessary to save the nation we love, or else those motivated by hatred will continue on this destructive path.

We have to understand that the basic principle driving these radicals is that the highest level of morality is actually having no morality. This is a difficult concept to understand; however, a failure to do so will always leave us one step behind. The Left is so completely dedicated to the creation of their "Utopian dream," or a "perfect world," if you will, that they believe there is no sin that isn't worth committing in order to achieve it. They believe that corrupting themselves in pursuit of this "perfect world" is in fact the highest level of morality one can achieve; they believe they are "self-sacrificing" for the cause. This is because their true belief revolves around the ideals of moral relativism; there is no absolute morality except for what they deem to be moral at the time. If the plundering of the economy in order to give the illusion that everybody is now equal pushes them towards their goal, then it is moral and just to do so because their end is an imagined paradise where everyone lives happily ever after.

It is next to impossible to fight this kind of ideology without 100 percent commitment from all who are willing to give it. Frankly, Americans have become far too complacent and comfortable to even acknowledge that the claims I am making are true. We have become adjusted, or conditioned, to believe that everything will continue on as it is. We are far too busy trying to maintain everything we believe we must have to notice the system which allows us to have these things slipping away. Perhaps many of us fell for the propaganda and believe that maybe things could be a little more equal. The only equality in Socialism and Communism is the equality of having absolutely nothing, my friends.

The Left has been chipping away at the very fabric of this nation for over one hundred years. Everyone on the Left is aware of the agenda and they are committed to its accomplishment, even if it means they go to their graves knowing their part was insignificant but necessary in the long run. For all practical purposes they are the epitome of the hive mentality. They are being driven by a hatred of everything we hold dear and they have been very successful. This is mainly because we fail to do what is necessary to stop them. They have employed Alinsky tactics masterfully as they use our own morality against us while they demonstrate that they have none. They know that as Christians we will not sink to the level of viciousness that they have, they know we will not tell the lies they do, they know we will not deliberately shame another in the name of accomplishing an agenda, and finally, they have learned that they can walk all over us and we will not fight back. America, if they are willing to tell lies and destroy this country while being motivated by hatred, isn't it time we ask ourselves what we are willing to do to save it based on the love we have for it? Think about it.

# 16

## Final Thoughts…

U pon the completion of this book, America finds herself still chugging along on the train of "fundamental transformation." As a result of the Ferguson incident, the Obama Administration has moved to nationalize local police forces. This is truly an alarming development, as anyone who has any true knowledge of history knows where this will lead.

Unfortunately, the division created by this administration has done its job, and very few are paying attention to the consequences of a liberal education system left unchecked. Thanks to the conditioning methods described in this book, students are literally unable to question what they are being taught, and feel compelled to sit quietly out of a fear of being singled out.

I remember sitting through many discussions about "white privilege" and asking my professor what the possible consequences of teaching this reverse racism could be. To me it was obvious that the ground work was being laid for the justification of what we are now witnessing in cities like Ferguson and Baltimore. This feeling was reinforced by fellow students who believed that they were indeed being oppressed by a society dominated by white men. I had heard on several occasions that the election of our first black president was hardly enough, and that a great deal more had to be done to make things right. The country is sitting on the edge of its seat in anticipation of what promises to be a summer filled with racial tensions, as President Obama seems intent on keeping anger focused on the police. Unfortunately, the only thing being accomplished is the reinforcement of a stereotype they claim to want to be rid of. Obama, and others on the left like Al Sharpton, are deliberately stoking the flames of racial hatred and as a result, they are doing nothing but creating criminals and destroying opportunity.

I have always wanted to believe that the ideals of liberty were something that would, in the end, unite Americans of all walks of life. I wanted to believe that whether we were black or white, Hispanic or Asian, we would see that we lived in a special place that provided us the freedom to be what we thought we were capable of being. After all let's face facts; no one is trying to escape the United States because she is an oppressive nation. On the contrary, people from around the world have risked a great deal for the opportunity to be the masters of their own lives, free of government control.

The Left has broken the human will to the point of dependency and as a result our lower natures can now be appealed to. Think about that a moment; the Left, in the Darwinist worldview, has attempted to teach us that we are not capable, and that we need someone "enlightened" to govern our daily affairs. As a result, the goals of ideological subversion have been realized; we as a society have lost the will to stand in the face of adversity.

Everything that we are experiencing in America is an all-out assault on the free will of mankind. Free will is a gift given to us by God; without it we will lose connection to him. Remember, one of Karl Marx's stated goals in the Communist Manifesto was the destruction of God in the minds of men. What we are engaged in is a spiritual war for the heart and soul of man, my friends. If this generation doesn't stand to take our nation back, it is highly unlikely the preceding generations will be able to.